The Word Encountered

The Word Encountered

Meditations on the Sunday Scriptures

John F. Kavanaugh, S.J.

ORBIS BOOKS

Maryknoll, New York 10545

Copyright © 1996 by John F. Kavanaugh, S.J.
Most of this book originally appeared in *America* magazine.
Published by Orbis Books, Maryknoll, NY 10545–0308

Manufactured in the United States of America

Library of Congress Cataloging-in-Publication Data

Kavanaugh, John F.
   The Word encountered : meditations on the Sunday Scriptures /
John F. Kavanaugh.
      p.   cm.
   ISBN 1-57075-093-9
   1. Church year sermons.   2. Catholic Church—Sermons.
3. Sermons, American.   I. Title.
BX1756.K356W67   1996
242'.3—dc20
                                                      96-13794
                                                          CIP

In Loving Memory of

Ann Manganaro
July 9, 1946–June 6, 1993
Sister of Loretto, Physician

and

Mev Puleo
January 26, 1963–January 12, 1996
Photo-Journalist, Theologian, Spouse of Mark Chmiel

Who so wondrously but so briefly
lived the Word in our midst

Contents

Preface   xi

1.   FIRST SUNDAY OF ADVENT
     Postponement and Repentance   1

2.   SECOND SUNDAY OF ADVENT
     Wastelands of Discontent   3

3.   THIRD SUNDAY OF ADVENT
     Gaudete: Rejoice   6

4.   FOURTH SUNDAY OF ADVENT
     This Is My Body   9

5.   CHRISTMAS AND HOLY FAMILY
     God Made Flesh   12

6.   MARY, MOTHER OF GOD, AND EPIPHANY
     First the Savor, Then the Sending   14

7.   BAPTISM OF THE LORD
     Transformations of the Body   15

8.   SECOND SUNDAY IN ORDINARY TIME
     The Body Sacred   17

9.   THIRD SUNDAY IN ORDINARY TIME
     Ambivalences of the Call   19

10.   FOURTH SUNDAY IN ORDINARY TIME
     Expressions of the Call   21

11.   FIFTH SUNDAY IN ORDINARY TIME
     The Ways of Jesus   22

12.   SIXTH SUNDAY IN ORDINARY TIME
     Living by Appearances   25

13. SEVENTH SUNDAY IN ORDINARY TIME
    The Paralysis of Unforgiven Guilt   28

14. EIGHTH SUNDAY IN ORDINARY TIME
    The New Law   30

15. NINTH SUNDAY IN ORDINARY TIME
    The Craft of Pharisees   32

16. TENTH SUNDAY IN ORDINARY TIME
    The Great Refusal   34

17. FIRST SUNDAY OF LENT
    Floods and Deserts   36

18. SECOND SUNDAY OF LENT
    Being Put to the Test   38

19. THIRD SUNDAY OF LENT
    Imperatives of Faith   41

20. FOURTH SUNDAY OF LENT
    Being Saved by God's Kind Favor   44

21. FIFTH SUNDAY OF LENT
    Repentance and Eucharist   47

22. PASSION SUNDAY
    Dying   49

23. EASTER SUNDAY
    Rising   51

24. SECOND SUNDAY OF EASTER
    Community Transformations   53

25. THIRD SUNDAY OF EASTER
    Glorified Bodies   56

26. FOURTH SUNDAY OF EASTER
    Other Sheep   59

27. FIFTH SUNDAY OF EASTER
    Radical Faith   61

28. SIXTH SUNDAY OF EASTER
    Hankering after the "Old Faith"   64

29. SEVENTH SUNDAY OF EASTER
    The Contest of Faith   67

30. PENTECOST
    Solidarity and Courage   69

31. TRINITY SUNDAY
    At the Bottom of Reality   72

32. BODY AND BLOOD OF CHRIST
    An Embodied God   75

33. ELEVENTH SUNDAY IN ORDINARY TIME
    Imperceptible Life   78

34. TWELFTH SUNDAY IN ORDINARY TIME
    Incomprehensible Death   80

35. THIRTEENTH SUNDAY IN ORDINARY TIME
    Prophetic Dying   82

36. FOURTEENTH SUNDAY IN ORDINARY TIME
    Prophetic Living   84

37. FIFTEENTH SUNDAY IN ORDINARY TIME
    The Burden of Baggage   85

38. SIXTEENTH SUNDAY IN ORDINARY TIME
    Jesus No Boy-O   87

39. SEVENTEENTH SUNDAY IN ORDINARY TIME
    The Bread of Life   89

40. EIGHTEENTH SUNDAY IN ORDINARY TIME
    The Bread of Labor   91

41. NINETEENTH SUNDAY IN ORDINARY TIME
    Sustained   93

42. TWENTIETH SUNDAY IN ORDINARY TIME
    Nurtured   94

43. TWENTY-FIRST SUNDAY IN ORDINARY TIME
Difficult Passages   96

44. TWENTY-SECOND SUNDAY IN ORDINARY TIME
Disturbing Words   98

45. TWENTY-THIRD SUNDAY IN ORDINARY TIME
"Faith, Yes, But . . ."   100

46. TWENTY-FOURTH SUNDAY IN ORDINARY TIME
Faith Doing Justice   101

47. TWENTY-FIFTH SUNDAY IN ORDINARY TIME
Perils of Power   103

48. TWENTY-SIXTH SUNDAY IN ORDINARY TIME
Perils of Wealth   106

49. TWENTY-SEVENTH SUNDAY IN ORDINARY TIME
The Two Shall Become as One   108

50. TWENTY-EIGHTH SUNDAY IN ORDINARY TIME
The Sadness of Many Securities   111

51. TWENTY-NINTH SUNDAY IN ORDINARY TIME
Lording It over the Rest   114

52. THIRTIETH SUNDAY IN ORDINARY TIME
The Terror of Love   116

53. THIRTY-FIRST SUNDAY IN ORDINARY TIME/ALL SAINTS DAY
Wholeheartedness of the Saints   119

54. THIRTY-SECOND SUNDAY IN ORDINARY TIME
When There Seems Nothing Left   122

55. THIRTY-THIRD SUNDAY IN ORDINARY TIME
The End Times   125

56. CHRIST THE KING
The King's Standard   128

Preface

Three years ago, at the invitation of Tom Stahel, from *America* magazine, I agreed to write a weekly column for that Jesuit-sponsored publication. "The Word," appearing at the end of each issue, is a reflection on the Sunday scriptures used for the liturgy of the Word. While the Fourth Gospel significantly appears every year, the "A," "B," and "C" cycles of readings feature Matthew, Mark, and Luke, respectively, over a run of three years.

The present collection is inspired by the readings for the "B" cycle, which starts once again at Advent in 1996. Stahel noted that, after three years, I might have something substantial to offer. If all goes well, by the time I end my tenure as a columnist for *America*, there will be three volumes for the three years of labor.

My own encounter with the scriptures has been profoundly influenced by my brothers in the Society of Jesus, whose company I entered at the age of eighteen. Since then, almost forty years ago, it has been their preaching and spiritual direction which has unlocked the word of God, whether in the elegant and measured phrasing of Charles Hunter or the intensity and fire of John Walsh and the late Vince O'Flaherty. Paul Quay over five years of spiritual direction helped me encounter the word of God with greater openness. In directed retreats Vince Hovley and Larry Gillick revealed the past promises and future glory as if we were on the road to Emmaus. John Foley brought the same lyrical grace to his preaching that was found in his music; John Schwantes, the luminous honesty of his conversation; Ed O'Brien, a mystical awe in the presence of the word and sacrament; Matt Ruhl, the sheer joy and energy of a living faith. Paul Reinert, well into his eighties, preached the word of God with wisdom and strength; Jay Alberg and Kevin Burke, half that age, always led the listener through the scriptures, with great hope and undying zeal.

To round out the appreciation I have for fellow Jesuits, I want to thank Father Philip Fischer for his careful and kind final editing suggestions, even those I may have been foolish enough not to follow. This work has been made far easier than it might have been by the close editing and computer wizardry of Bob Collins at *America*. It is through the kind graces of that Jesuit apostolate that I am able to offer this token of gratitude for the Word made flesh.

1. Postponement and Repentance

Is. 63:16–19; 64:2–7; 1 Cor. 1:3–9; Mk. 13:33–37

"We are sinful, unclean people."

As a child, I thought that Advent was an artificial thing. It seemed a forced time of year, a concoction to get us excited about the coming of Christmas. It felt fake.

After all, the birth of Christ had happened a long time ago. What was the point of pretending that it hadn't? It was like going through the motions of contrived expectancy when we knew the outcome in advance.

Now I am beginning to see Advent differently. The cycle of the seasons that we as a worshiping people live through each year is not an exercise in "let's pretend" at all. It is an ongoing journey into deeper reality. It is a recognition that the entry of God into our lives, while ontologically accomplished, is still psychologically unfinished.

As long as we breathe, there is more of our lives to open, to unbar, to unlock. There is always more of us that we might let God enter. There is no end to the ways that the Word of God can more fully take on our flesh.

This is especially true of our need to acknowledge how utterly we rely on God's healing power for our salvation. We so much want to be whole and finished that our greatest temptation is to think and hope the task is done. Oh, if this conversion could only be our last. If this long journey of faith could be neat, final, and complete.

Embarrassed as we all are at the wounds we bear and the scars hidden at the bottom of our being, we only reluctantly admit our vulnerability. We would rather not be reminded,

1

once again, of our need for redemption. Far more tempting is escape. Far more appealing is the prospect that we can sleep-walk through life and not address the pain.

The words of Jesus in the Gospel of Mark may be read not only as a warning about the end times, but as a challenge for us to live in the present, to engage life now, to be attentive to the moment at hand. It is the call of Advent itself. Be awake. Do not put off the opening of your life to God.

Denial and postponement are especially true in the matter of our sins, those wounds that we somehow inflict upon ourselves and others. Repression of the truth is common. Admission and reform are rare. We project, we accuse, we complain, we evade, we distract ourselves. We are not as adept at confession.

In our own place and time, we have made a science of escape and sleep. Rather than live at that sharp edge of life, awake and alert, we pretend that we have no sin. There is nothing wrong with me, no change required of us. Others need the help. My coworkers, my friends and community, my family are to blame. "Evil empires," "warlords" and "endless enemies" are the source of our problems. Bishops or feminists, conservatives or leftists, liberation theologians or curial despots are the favorite demons of choice.

We in the church are not especially noted for our willingness to confess our own sins and welcome repentance. At best, one part of the church will attack the other. But how uncommon it is to hear theologians acknowledge the sinfulness of the theologian—unless it is a theologian of the opposite persuasion. How scarce is the hierarchy's confession of guilt. How unusual it is to hear the right wing warn us of conservatives' sins. How rare is the liberal who admits the possible disorders of liberalism.

Every Eucharist, like every Advent, begins with a call for repentance and a plea for mercy. But how real is it for us? How awake, how open are we to the truth of our inadequacy and the entrance of God into our lives? How willing are we to make the words of Isaiah our own? "Why do you let us wander from your ways and harden our hearts so that we fear you not? We are sinful, unclean people, our good deeds like polluted rags. We have been delivered up to guilt."

What a hierarchy, what a priesthood, what a people of God we would be if we allowed such sentiments to be our own. But we recoil from the implications. They would have us change. They would make a difference in the way we look at the world. They would unmask too many of the pretenses and postures we have assumed.

The theme of Advent is not "let's pretend." It is "get real." Here. Now. Make real the need for God. Make real God's entry. Make real the word—not just as a text or a story, but as a disclosure of truth. Not only is God revealed to us. You and I, here and now, are revealed to ourselves.

Thus, every Advent is an opportunity. Together, we might once again experience the Word of God taking flesh in us. And having allowed God such profound entry, we may find ourselves giving birth anew to the Word in our world.

2. Wastelands of Discontent

Is. 40:1–5, 9–11; 2 Pet. 3:8–14; Mk. 1:1–8

"Comfort, give comfort to my people."

A few years ago, *Forbes* magazine, that font of capitalist wisdom, entitled its seventy-fifth anniversary issue "Why We Feel so Bad When We Have It so Good." It sported articles by some of the media luminaries of our time: Peggy Noonan, writer for Ronald Reagan, George Bush, and Dan Rather; the brilliant novelist John Updike, who reminded us of lawyers' gorgeous fees, "like a black hole at the center of the business world, sucking dollars into it," and the greed of corporate heads "who with giant salaries and rigged deals looted their companies as shamelessly as Third World dictators looted their impoverished countries"; the Nobel laureate Saul Bellow, writing of the disillusionment that comes from our cultural fascination with affluence; and the historian Gertrude Himmelfarb, warning us of the weary discontent haunting a nation surprised to discover that "economic and material goods are no compensation for social and moral ills."

In so many ways we are a disconsolate people, members of a "joyless" economy whose models of fashion and rock stare with sullen eyes and false rage. We turn on ourselves in violence. Witness the geometric rises in homicide and suicide rates, the murder of our unborn by the millions and the moral disenfranchisement of our young. Our very lives seem so externalized, so bereft of intrinsic value, that the technology of ending them has become alluring. The prospect of a Dr. Kevorkian to extinguish the pain or a Derek Humphry to ease our "final exit" is a deadly theme of half-serious jokes.

We may be an attractive people, Peggy Noonan mused, but we are somehow terribly sad. We have been formed as a people to expect happiness endlessly, but the search has caused only more misery. She links this to a deep cultural belief that this world is the only existence there is, our only chance to be happy, and "If that is what you believe, then you are not disappointed when the world does not give you a good measure of its riches, you are despairing."

It is the despair of exile—from one's homeland and one's self—that is addressed in Second Isaiah's "Book of Consolation." And if the prophet's is a living word, it speaks not only to a people over twenty-five centuries ago. It confronts us. This is what it means to appropriate holy scripture as our own: not a disembodied historical text, but a message that penetrates our own reality.

Certainly this encounter is appropriate for a community of faith bearing the very name of the Word made flesh and inhabiting countries whose national spirits were once influenced by the God of Moses and the prophets as well as the Father of Jesus.

We let voices cry out in our own wastelands: Isaiah calling us to prepare a way for the Lord, the writer of 2 Peter asking us to come to repentance, John the Baptizer proclaiming "a baptism which led to the forgiveness of sins."

The happy paradox of it all is that repentance itself is the beginning of hope. The moment we recognize our insufficiency and failure, we can own up to our exiled condition, from which we long to return. Sin's acknowledgment is the birth of renewal. Even more, as men and women of faith, we affirm that the longing born of repentance will not go unanswered by a God who would have us "fear not," who would shepherd us, carry us, gather us into loving arms. God wants none of us to perish, no good of us to be lost. As the spirituality of Alcoholics Anonymous reveals, the admission of our unmanageable exile invites us to hope for "one more powerful yet to come."

Thus we cannot save ourselves. We know we are not the Messiah. But in the promise that has been given, in the covenant that has been offered, we can find our voice and speak once again the truth that the great ones before us like Isaiah and the Baptizer have given to our ancestors.

It was Lee Atwater, maker of presidents, inventor of "kicking butt" and Willie Horton campaigns, hobnobber with rock stars, who—finally brought low by the ravages of brain cancer— spoke most forcefully to a people that had given itself over to the illusions of power, wealth, and prestige.

In "Lee Atwater's Last Campaign" (*Life,* February 1991), he revealed his anguish, not over his own fate but over the fate of our age—our moral decay, our exile from love, our loss of compassion and friendship. He seemed to search for voices that would be raised in hope despite our own wilderness. "I don't know who will lead us through the '90s, but they must be made to speak to this spiritual vacuum at the heart of American society, this tumor of the soul."

Who will do this, if not those who know their own vulnerability and sinfulness? Who, if not those who have hope in the providence of God and the possibility of reform in the human heart? Who, if not us?

3. Gaudete: Rejoice

Is. 61:1–2, 10–12; 1 Thess. 5:16–24; Jn. 1:6–8, 19–28

"I am not the Messiah."

Among the many ways we might receive the word of God, we can hear and read it in the context of its presumed original setting. Thus Isaiah's beautiful prophecy of glad tidings to the poor, healing for the broken-hearted, and liberty to captives is the likely promise of restoration of homeland and freedom to an exiled and defeated ancient people.

We could also investigate the word from the point of view of the author and the author's audience. This could be our focus, whether we investigate the historical situation of the Hebrew people and the actual time a prophecy was recorded or look into the matter of this prophecy's presence in the Gospel of Luke, when Jesus reveals his ministry in Nazareth's synagogue. No matter what might have been on Jesus' mind and lips, the use of Isaiah was certainly in the minds and hearts of the early church's articulation of its encounter with Christ.

A third level of our engagement, a third type of focus, is presented by the context of our own lives and times: how we receive and respond. In some ways, it is this focus which is so difficult to hold. For if we allow ourselves to stand unmasked and unguarded before the Word of God, we may be shaken, transformed, and winnowed.

It might well seem safer to read and hear the gospel as if it all applied to something that happened long ago. We are willing to stop at its historical meanings or its dogmatic implications. But that is not the full range of its voice. It is spoken to us here and now.

That is why Jesus' use of the Isaiah passage in the fourth chapter of Luke is particularly suggestive. After he gave the scroll back and all eyes were fixed on him, he said, "This text is being fulfilled today even as you listen." It is fulfilled in our own hearing of it. Thus we are the Israelites receiving the promise that God will make "justice and praise spring up before all the nations." We are the Thessalonians "waiting for the coming of the Lord," advised not to stifle the Spirit or despise prophecies. We must in some way make John the Baptizer's words our own.

It is rather easy to objectify and externalize God's voice in the world. The poor, the broken-hearted, the blind, the captives were back then and out there. But Jesus insisted that Isaiah's words were not merely for previous generations. They were for the present. They are for our present.

Even if we accept his words, however, for the present time, we still have a struggle to take them to heart. Perhaps we presume that the broken-hearted of our world must be healed; perhaps we think we ought to work for prison reform; perhaps we imagine ourselves challenged to work for the poor. But this is still not the deepest point of revelation.

For the prophecy is fulfilled in my, in our, very receiving of it addressed to us. It is you and I who are the poor. We are impoverished, not only in the matters of our unfulfilled desires, material or otherwise, but in the more secret matters of our personal vulnerability, our inability to save and heal ourselves, our utter incapacity to manage our way through life and love.

And it is we too who suffer broken hearts in those very lives and loves and labors that mark our existence. There is no woman, man, or child I have ever met who has been exempt from this condition. There are many of us, however, who have repressed or ignored that very fact. The receiving of the prophecy is the recognition of our truth.

So it is with our blindness before grace, to the bounty of life, to the gift of each breath and movement of our hearts. So also with our inability to see the wounds and gifts of those near and far. We have eyes but see not.

We too are captive: prisoners of barred rooms and closed roads, unable to see our way out of failure, our betrayals and egoisms, our fears that paralyze, our attachments that hold us frozen.

So is this church captive, sinful and poor, broken and held in thrall by its own idols and obsessions. Let us count the ways.

And so also our nations are caught in nationalisms, our tribes trapped in tradition that crushes human life and spirit, our economic and political classes locked in vested interest.

As we hear the word sounded or read it written, let it first "be fulfilled in our hearing of it." O God, be with us, be our Emmanuel. Come to our poor inadequacy. Open our tired eyes. Free us—all of us. Unlock our hearts and minds.

If we do not encounter the Word of God on this most primary and existential level, all the historical reflections of human hermeneutics will not move us. All the high speculative theologies in the world will not transform our hearts.

We must, in effect, take upon ourselves the attitude of the Baptizer; one thing I know for sure: "I am not the Messiah."

4.   This Is My Body

2 Sam. 7:1–5, 8–11, 16; Rom. 16:25–27; Lk. 1:26–38

"Nothing is impossible with God."

Where is the proper place for God to abide? Where can we find the Most High? Perhaps these were the questions that David asked of himself and his adviser Nathan, because the king was disturbed to be living in a cedar palace while God's ark was confined in a tent. Although Nathan assured David that God was with him no matter where he might go, it was only Nathan's night-time revelation from God that could make the case: "Why should you build a house for me? I have been with you no matter where you have been. And I will build an even greater house for you."

What are these readings getting at? What is the mystery— "hidden for many ages," Paul writes in Romans—that is now manifested through Jesus? What is the upshot of this talk of God's temple and dwelling place—especially in the light of Advent and the promise of Christmas?

The pre-infancy narrative in Luke provides the central clue. It may even suggest a paradoxical answer to one of the more troublesome issues in our contemporary church.

Mary is told by the angel Gabriel, the messenger of God, that the Lord is with her. Much more intimate than God's presence to David, the Lord is literally with her. She is the dwelling place. She is the new ark, beyond all our reasonable expectations. She is tent and temple. God is literally, physically in her, conceived as human, her very flesh, great with dignity, by the power of the Most High. And she is the temple. She is the greater house, the promise to David.

"Let it be done to me according to your word."

It is Mary's very acceptance of the "mystery hidden for ages," her utter openness to the promise of God's intimacy with us, that yields her pregnancy. She believed that God could take human flesh in her, become one with her very body. Herein, she was fertile to bear forth the Most High into the world.

This is the heart of the Incarnation mystery: that the ineffable and unnameable God could take human flesh, could become one with us, could be a human baby.

Her "yes," her "fiat," is, of course, momentous in the drama of the world, an axial point of history. The willingness of Mary to open her life utterly to God is a model of our humanity as well as of our church and sacraments.

And this is what brings us to a conundrum of our times.

How does Mary reveal the place of women in the "Mystical Body of Christ"? How do women fit into the church?

We have called Mary not only the mother of Jesus, but the "mother" of divine grace, most pure, inviolate and undefiled. We have termed her amiable, admirable, counselor, prudent, venerable, most powerful, merciful, and faithful. She is the mirror of justice, seat of wisdom, singular vessel of devotion, the tower of David. She is the house of gold, a gate of heaven, healer of the sick, a refuge of sinners, and comforter of the afflicted.

Does not a question suggest itself? If Mary—the mother of Jesus Christ, the very Word of God made flesh—is all of that, could she be a priest?

There are those who think that women should be ordained. There are those who think otherwise. But who among them appeals to the revelation of Christ, rather than enlightened self-interest, merely human traditions, or ideology? Who among them humbly considers the Word of God, willing to say, "Let it be done according to your word"?

Blessed Isaac of Stella, in the readings of the Liturgy of the Hours for Saturday of the second week of Advent, portrays the reality of Mary that we must all assume.

In a way, every Christian is also believed to be a bride of God's Word, a mother of Christ, His daughter and sister, at once virginal and fruitful. These words are used in a universal sense of the church, in a special sense of Mary, in a particular sense of the individual Christian. . . . Christ dwelt for nine months in the tabernacle of Mary's womb. He dwells until the end of the ages in the tabernacle of the church's faith.

This observation of Blessed Isaac is a challenge to those of us who might think that a woman does not appropriately image Christ or adequately symbolize the incarnate mystery.

The Blessed Virgin Mary was the first human person who could say of Jesus, "This is my body, this is my blood." She was the first altar of the Incarnation's mystery. Her body a fitting temple, she was the prime analogate for those who know and live the mysteries of transubstantiation.

Was she not, then, the first priest, the first minister of the sacrament of the real presence?

How might those who hold that women are symbolically inadequate for the priesthood think about this? What might some feminists, who seem only ashamed of Mary, the mother of God, find by entering the mystery of her being? What might we all learn of her utter openness to the presence of God? That we, too, are called to make the Word our flesh?

5. God Made Flesh

Is. 9:1–6; Tit. 2:11–14; Lk. 2:1–14
Sir. 3:2–6, 12–14; Col. 3:12–21; Lk. 2:22–40

"You have nothing to fear!"

If anything, Christianity—and especially Catholicism—takes human flesh seriously. Our central mystery is the Incarnation—God's "enfleshment," the necessary condition for the life and teachings of Jesus, his redemptive death, and his glorious resurrection.

God marries our human flesh and finiteness. In Jesus the eternal Word of God becomes wombed in time. Thus, we who bear his name and live his life are a people who see the transcendent in the particularities of names, places, historical events.

To others, our faith and practice may seem embarrassingly concrete and physical.

I remember a non-Christian woman, after weighing the possibility of becoming Catholic, saying to me, "But it seems all so primitive, so fleshy."

It is strange, when you think of it. We celebrate conceptions, circumcisions, and purifications; we ritualize marriage so highly that some of those who have left our communion are struck by the leanness, even barrenness, of some other marriage ceremonies. Births and deaths we linger and pray and play over. Food and blood characterize our Eucharists.

It is unsettling for many—and sometimes for us—that God would penetrate and inhabit our ordinariness. It might be more reassuring if our Baby-God had sprung fully matured from the head of Zeus, instead of appearing in the midst of such inadequacy and vulnerability. Sure, we have the angels, but they tell us merely to "fear not." And they point, like the star, to things so utterly undramatic and common as a makeshift bed and plain people.

Even early pseudodocuments of Jesus' birth and childhood seem uncomfortable with the common condition of the "baby Jesus." They would have this infant more splendiferous, this child more ominously powerful, someone shooting lightning bolts from his fingers.

And yet the plain humanity of Christmas is what it is all about, our lives and God's. In the last analysis we are as defenseless as a child before the great forces of time and consciousness. What is more, we are reminded that our very God, as well, is somehow like a child, defenseless before us. Perhaps that is why the heavenly advice so often given in the infancy narratives is "fear not."

It is fitting that the holiness of the family also be celebrated at this time. For it is only by the ordinariness of being born, nurtured, and taught, so frail and dependent upon those who have welcomed us into their lives, that we ever grow in strength and grace.

God enters these intimacies, too, just as surely as God wants entry into all of human history. And so the wisdom of the father and the authority of the mother and reverence of the child reveal the splendor. Sometimes the wise old ones in our midst, like Simeon, help us name the glory. Other times, it is the prophetic ancient, like Anna, who sees the truth of our ordinary radiance.

Paul reminds us that the virtues of daily life—kindness, thankfulness, patience, and forbearance—embody our good and gracious God, who has willed to dwell in us. Our submission to each other, our love, our care lest the frail among us lose heart, is the making, once again, of the Word into our flesh.

6.   First the Savor, Then the Sending

Num. 6:22–27; Gal. 4:4–7; Lk. 2:16–21
Is. 60:1–6; Eph. 3:2–6; Mt. 2:1–12

"Mary treasured all these things."

My father, a year before he died, said to me (I thought), "It's amazing how fast the year goes by."

It was late spring, and my term of teaching was closing out, so it was easy to agree. "Yes, I can't believe it's April already. I hardly know my students' names."

"No," he said, "not this year. The years. I can't believe how fast the last thirty years went."

His wife, a few years later, offered her own observation about the passing of time. A young mother of three seemed to ask her, "Isn't it wonderful, now that you have time to do all the things you want without all the demands and rush of a growing family?"

"No," my mother said. "I would be perfectly happy to have those kids running around, especially if I could see then what I see now. But now is also good, and I'm going to appreciate it all while it's still here."

Sometimes the years seem to hurtle by. There are those days when I, my parents' child, wonder: How do I let it all get away so fast? How can I hold on to it better? How can I see it better?

Well, at least numbering the years helps. Like birthdays and the change of seasons, the marking of a New Year invites us to remembrance and recollection. We all could learn a thing or two from that old religious practice of singing the *Te Deum* on December 31: a day to thank God for all the days, a moment to bless all the moments of mind and heart, breath and sight. A time to "see" and savor.

It is our celebration of Mary, the mother of God, who "treasured all these things and reflected on them in her heart," that starts our new year. And the gospel tells us of shepherds who took time to approach the mystery and wondrously saw Mary and Joseph and the child. "Once they saw, they understood."

Even the ancient feast of the Epiphany celebrates our seeing, our witnessing of the mystery that God could take our very flesh and bones. In the light of the Incarnation, with the "showing" of God in Jesus, all is changed, all human ordinariness transformed, all of the commonplace transfigured and blessed.

A sense of how God "shows" in each day, how grace is manifest in every numbered year, allows us to take possession of our moments gently as time flashes by. We develop a richer taste for life itself, and our thanksgiving reaches deeper into our being.

If we fully enter into the revelation of Christmas, if we truly savor it and thereby savor the lives we've been gifted with, we may find ourselves joining the long march of witnesses, sent to all times and nations, to bestow the blessing of God that the Book of Numbers gave to us: "The Lord bless you and keep you. The Lord's face shine upon you and be gracious to you. The Lord look kindly upon you and give you peace."

BAPTISM OF THE LORD

7. Transformations of the Body

Is. 42:1–4, 6–7; Acts 10:34–38; Mk. 1:7–11

"My beloved."

Why was Jesus baptized? Even for the early church, as the canon of scripture itself was being formed, it seems to have been a controversial question. If Jesus goes before John for the "baptism of repentance," it seems that Jesus himself is a sinner. The account from the Gospel of Matthew suggests as much when giving voice to John's reluctance: "It is I who need baptism from you, and yet you come to me!"

Mark's Gospel begins with John's proclamation, "for the forgiveness of sins," and the promise that "someone greater than I is to come." The next moment, we see the "someone," whose sandal straps John is not worthy to untie, receiving the sign of repentance from John, not giving it.

It is not only a special irony. It is a central image of the redemptive mystery. Jesus enters into radical solidarity with all men and women, taking upon himself even the condition of our sinfulness, himself having not sinned. The "one more powerful" assumes the position of weakness. It is precisely in this that he is beloved. And it is from this baptism sign that he is sent.

He was like us in all things but sin, the author of Hebrews reminds us when discussing Jesus' high priesthood. And yet we balk at the statement. "If he did not sin, how could he really be like us? How could he be fully human?"

We misunderstand this because we misunderstand our humanity as well as our sin. Christ has come not only to reveal the divinity to us; he has come to reveal us to ourselves. Not only is he truly God. He is truly human. And he is truly human precisely because he does not sin. All of our sin is nothing other than the rejection of the truth of our humanity. Jesus' utter acceptance of our humanity, his drinking of our cup fully, his sharing of our wounded condition, reverses our sinful rejection of our creatureliness.

His baptism, then, is at the heart of his mission to heal us. He enters even the wounds of our self-rejection, without having made the rejection himself. He accepts full solidarity with us even if it means being seen as sinner. Jesus' baptism is one of his earliest great transformations of our human condition. The first was that the Word itself could take human flesh. All the further implications would follow: that he would be tempted to reject this mission of transformation; that he would undertake all manner of healing and disarming of devils; that he would announce a kingdom to transmute all blindness, poverty, imprisonment, and darkness;

that he would, at last, suffer the very fate of sin in death.

Just as we now baptize our children to announce a new fate for the human body, the baptism of Jesus is the inauguration of that fate. Announced as sinner, wholly one with our condition, Jesus, hovered over by the very spirit of God, is gazed upon by the Father who sent him and who now says to him—and all of us who share his flesh—"This is my beloved, in whom I am well pleased."

8. The Body Sacred

1 Sam. 3:3–10, 19; 1 Cor. 6:13–15, 17–20; Jn. 1:35–42

"Come and see."

If we ask God to speak to us in Christ, if we wish to abide with him, he simply tells us to follow, to look, and to hear.

Should we do so, however, all things will look different.

Paul does not let us escape this fact. In the transforming mission of Jesus, even our bodies will look different. If God can inhabit human flesh, it cannot be made for immorality. If our bodies are temples of God, we must not desecrate them. They are, Paul says, the very glory of God.

This is difficult for us today. How dare someone tell us "You are not your own"? We pride ourselves on autonomy. Our bodies are our property, there for our use or abuse, our pleasure or management, ours to begin or end at will.

And yet the body is a big problem for us, whether we want to admit it or not. Even the late, great psychologist Abraham Maslow, no churchly or Pauline preacher to say the least, warned us of the body's degradation in our time. In his essay "Self-actualization and Beyond," what he said of youth could be said of all of us:

> [They] have learned to reduce the person to the concrete
> object and to refuse to see what he might be or to refuse
> to see him in his symbolic values or to refuse to see him
> or her eternally. [They] have desacralized sex, for example.
> Sex is nothing; it is a natural thing, and they have made it
> so natural that it has lost its poetic qualities in many
> instances, which means that it has lost practically every-
> thing. Self-actualization means giving up this defense
> mechanism and learning or being taught to resacralize.

Say what we may about the differing meanings for "fornica-
tion" in the first century and our own, try as we might to
deflate Paul's challenge as a form of Manichaeism and rejection of the body, the practice of human sexuality in contemporary culture is in no way worthy of a temple.

Familiar statistics reveal that more than one-half of our
youth have had intercourse by the age of seventeen, and half
of their pregnancies end in abortion. Births to unmarried teens
have risen 200 percent between 1960 and 1980. Chlamydia,
genital warts, herpes, gonorrhea, and syphilis have increased,
despite the doubling of condom use among teenagers in the
last ten years. Stories of sexual violence against women and
the abuse of children fill our network news and our newspapers. One estimate is that a woman is raped every six minutes
in the United States. One of the most frequently used words
for women in low rap music on MTV is the same that once
rarely was heard applied to a female dog. And the September
1992 *Vogue* magazine featured a sleazy article called "Chain
Reactions" about sadism—photographer Helmut Newton with
a gaudy photograph of a topless, bound woman, nipples
pierced, pointing a gun to her head. A caption read, "Making a
virtue out of vice."

Maslow would wince.

St. Paul, for his part, has already advised us: We are called to
a different way. We heed a different voice. And we look at the
human body as a temple, transformed by the eyes of faith.

9. Ambivalences of the Call

Jon. 3:1–10; 1 Cor. 7:29–31; Mk. 1:14–20

"Come after me."

It is a common misunderstanding, it seems to me, to expect that the experience of a call from God is somehow laced with peace, charged with happiness, and results in victory. Most instances in the scriptures suggest otherwise. Many prophets, even Moses, were reluctant and hesitant. They often felt not up to the test at all. Sometimes they regretted that the call had ever been placed.

Jonah's problem was even more confounding. He was invested with a momentous message for the sprawling city of Nineveh. The entire place was going to be demolished by God in forty days' time.

And yet, before Jonah could walk through the city announcing its doom, the whole lot of them, including the king, repented. Moved by their change of heart, their sackcloth and ashes, God relented and did not execute the threat.

What's interesting—only if you read beyond the ten lines used for this Sunday's readings—is that Jonah gets very upset. In fact, he's enraged and embarrassed: "I might as well be dead as go on living."

He should have known better, Jonah admits, even at the moment of the call. The message was clear and he gave it, but his worst suspicions concerning God's tenderness were confirmed. His predictions would not come true. The only bright spot: Nineveh was saved. God asks: "Am I not to feel sorry for Nineveh, the great city, in which there are more than a hundred and twenty thousand people who cannot tell their right hand from their left, to say nothing of all the animals?"

(Jon. 4:11). Thank God the heart of God is not like the egos of those he calls.

As much can be said of the apostles whom Jesus called to himself. By all rational accounts, they were a chancy lot. And their subsequent doubts would seem to number as many as their confirmations.

You would think that, after being invited by one such as Christ, all would be smooth sailing. Things would be free and clear. They would have one confirmation after another. And yet, we know their call must surely have been experienced as a journey into frustration and failure.

How many setbacks can one experience and yet not question the call in the first place? How many hopes, once clung to, have to be given up, before you give up?

Perhaps the words of St. Paul are responsive to these questions, when he advises radical detachment from every cherished good. Business, family, feelings, all indeed lovely—all messages from God's bounty—but none of them is God's very self. No one of these lavish gifts is the giver.

We are all, in effect, pilgrims, prophets, apostles, and sojourners in this passing bright circus of the world. We all have our message to give and our own act to perform. Such is the nature of our call into existence.

But like Jonah, we are well advised not to let immediate expectations or even our long-range dreams delude us. In the end, the final word is Good News from this strangely wonderful God who wants to capture us all in a net of eternal love.

10. Expressions of the Call

Dt. 18:15–20; 1 Cor. 7:32–35; Mk. 1:21–28

"I am going into this for your own good."

The reading from Corinthians will probably infuriate its share of people. In a day and age when many of us are loath to admit any differences between religious life, clerical life, and the life of the laity, here comes Paul, shoulders and all, barging into our liturgy with these outrageous statements.

To top it off, he says it's for our own good.

He offends just about everyone. Top of the list: me. As if to suggest that my life—childless, spouseless—is free of worries. We all know, as a matter of fact, that unmarried men and women can be the all-time best worriers. And there is ample evidence that celibacy and virginity guarantee neither single-minded service nor whole-hearted devotion to the Lord.

On the other hand, I continue to get reports, even complaints, that the last thing a husband is concerned with is pleasing his wife—or the wife her husband, for that matter.

In a nutshell, who can doubt that among married people are numbered some of the holiest people we know? And, among priests and religious, who has not found people capable of prodigious mediocrity? Or worse.

The point is, I really do not think that St. Paul is claiming something so boldly counterintuitive.

Certainly an unmarried person devoted to God will have more time for service of others, especially on an emergency basis, and also have more time for quiet and isolated prayer. All mothers and fathers I have ever known, immersed in the demands of labor and family, have in some way sighed for the time to do such things.

But the crucially operative word is "devoted to God." If that is not there, all the "worryless" free time in the world will not yield a thimbleful of love. And as Paul has written elsewhere, with "devotedness to God" even the most ordinary experiences of parenting, family, and spousal love can be astounding revelations of God's grace and intimacy in our lives.

I do believe, however, that Paul is getting at something more. It is this: When I look at my brother's life—his spouse and children, his business and profession, his endless tasks involved just with house and automobile—I am utterly convinced that he reveals an encounter and intimacy with God that I never could. It is not necessarily higher or lower. But it is thoroughly different, marvelously diverse in contrast to my life.

But I also believe that a single person, whether lay or religious or priest, reveals by his or her life a dimension of God's love and grace that a married person quite simply does not. To say the least, it reveals the possibility of a love which is greater than the loveliest gifts of this earth, a love through which all our earthly loves move and toward which all are drawn.

And surely Paul would agree: If such a life is not, indeed, grounded in God, what a terrible waste it shall have been.

FIFTH SUNDAY IN ORDINARY TIME

11. The Ways of Jesus

Job 7:1–4, 6–7; 1 Cor. 9:16–19, 22–23; Mk. 1:29–39

"For the sake of the gospel."

We do not have to feel the drudgery and anguish of Job to sense sometimes that our lives are without point or passion.

While disaster and depression might be rare for us, ennui and a lack of focus are not. And they are enough to bring us low. The causes can be many, yet often enough it is just simply a "managerial" attitude toward our lives, a "maintenance" frame of mind, that makes our feelings and faith go flat. We seriously misunderstand our faith if we see it in terms of getting by and getting through. If that is what it is all about, it has to become a frightful bore.

Perhaps at times our young people catch this. They sense a tedium, a staleness about our religion and our practices. "Mass is so boring," a young woman recently told me. Well, surely, she is not going to find much entertainment there—especially if you compare it to our fifty available channels and the razzmatazz of pop culture. And besides, why would one expect novelty and slickness from a sacred communal practice, the hallmarks of which are great tradition, universality, and stability of form?

But I also think my young friend is on to something. There is not much intensity or urgency in a community whose primary concerns are managing its relationship to God and maintaining its own existence. Is the church really about the powerful message of Christ, or is it just concerned with itself?

St. Paul, on the other hand, seems positively driven to write and speak of Jesus and his revelation. "I am under compulsion and have no choice. I am ruined if I do not preach it!" So much does his faith mean to him that he is willing to be the slave of all, to be all things to all people in order to win them over. For Paul, the faith is definitely not a matter of small consequence.

We, in contrast, seem hounded by doubts. Is it really that big a deal that people believe in Jesus? Does it matter very much to us if our children drift away from a faith we say we love? Isn't one religion just as good as another? And don't theologians themselves suggest that conversions, missions, and proselytism are passé, if not wrong-headed?

Well, if our faith is something that really does not make a very big difference, if it is actually not crucial that we or others believe, no wonder it seems boring to some of our young.

Anything we don't care much about can't be very interesting.

The things we do care about, however, we inevitably talk about. As another, very wise, young person put it: "If you love someone or something deeply enough, you want to tell others, you want to share it with others, you think they are missing something if they do not have it."

Paul's drivenness is as understandable as the lover's. Both turn almost desperately to declamation, poetry, or song.

If faith is real, it seeks expression. It will communicate and profess. It will have the energy of passion.

But faith cannot be real for us if it is not allowed into our real world. A Christ who is squeezed into a pew may feel cozy, but the relationship will soon tire and confine.

Could this be one of the reasons why the Gospel of Mark at the outset portrays our encounters with Christ over a broad range of life experiences?

We first find Jesus leaving the synagogue to enter into the midst of human intimacies—friends, community, and family. He walks and abides with comrade-apostles and their in-laws. There he is found. He inhabits relationship.

Second, he is never far from pain and diminishment. Grasping the hand of Simon's mother-in-law, he helps her up as her fever abates. Other people with afflictions, obsessions, and interior injuries call out for his touch and he responds. This was not his major work, of course, but he seemed always to have time for the marginal and the outsider.

Third, he is found in the "lonely place." Mark notes here that the desert is where he finds solitude. At other times, it is on the mountain. But as it is with his appearance in relationships and the wounded of the world, he maintains this dimension of quiet and prayer as a hallmark of his life.

The ground of the real world—our solitude, our relationships, and our human solidarity—is the terrain from which Jesus sets out to proclaim the good news and visit the synagogues of Galilee.

Our practice of faith, our discipleship, cannot be otherwise.

Jesus not only transforms our secluded moments, our intimacies, and our social compassion. He lives there.

And his presence is a matter of supreme importance. For in our human solitude we find not isolated brokenness—we discover a citadel of relationship to God. Our friends are not diversions from a far-off deity; they give our life in God flesh and blood. The call of the wounded is not merely some problem to solve or avoid; it is an invitation to love's redemptive power.

The Eucharist re-enacts this truth. And without this truth or its expression, we would be, like Paul if he were not to preach Christ, quite desperate.

12. Living by Appearances

Lev. 13:1–2, 44–46; 1 Cor. 10:31–11:1; Mk. 1:40–45

"Unclean, unclean!"

Pimples. Boils. Ugliness. Wrinkles. Fat. Sores. Open wounds. Rashes. Blotches. Blemishes. Disfigurement.

The thought of such afflictions can be particularly unnerving—especially in a culture that lives by appearances and first impressions. Although quite possibly every culture prizes the surface of things, ours seems to have made a science of the old advertising slogan: "Looking good is everything."

Looking bad is disastrous. It is the fate of the outsider, the face of the other, marginalized and excluded. Surface defects seem inescapable, since our appearances are so evident and immediate.

Our presentation, our appearance, to the outside world is the only way we get out, the only way we can reveal ourselves. And yet our external presentation itself can be a barrier that holds us in as it holds others away.

Perhaps this is the secret to the power of leper stories. "Leper" seems so frightening a term to begin with, we almost never hear it anymore, but for the mentionings in holy scripture.

Be that as it may, it is most likely that the Hebrew *sara'at* and Greek *lepra,* which are translated as "leprosy," do not describe the condition that has become known as Hansen's disease. The affliction referred to in the Bible is, rather, always a condition of visible defect, whether on human skin, on the walls of houses, or on fabrics and leather. It is a disorder of surfaces, a superficial disfigurement, a blemish of facades. And it never seems to go away.

The visibility of it all makes social exclusion easy. Its persistent presence makes contamination a constant threat. "As long as the sore is on him, he shall declare himself unclean, since he is in fact unclean. He shall dwell apart, making his abode outside the camp."

Surface defects are readily found out. There is no way to hide them, unless one hides oneself. Pretense does not help. Denial is impossible. It is right out there. The only thing to do is accept the condition.

Perhaps this is an advantage that the visibly handicapped have over those whose handicaps are hidden. At least they know they have the problem: It's inescapable. At least they cannot pretend: It's undeniable. At least they know that there is room for healing in their lives. Admission of the truth is the first condition for change.

"If you will to do so, you can cure me." "I do will it. Be cured."

A paradox of our faith is that it requires of us a frame of mind we are least comfortable with: an acceptance of our existential disabilities. Not only are we unable to save ourselves. We are profoundly blemished. And all the makeup in the world cannot do the trick.

We may even someday wish to present ourselves to God as spotless milk bottles, clean, whole, pasteurized, and uncontaminated: a sad delusion. For not only is the aspiration impossible; the whole point of Christ's redemptive life is missed.

The gospel invites us to enter the mystery of our own disabilities, hidden or otherwise. We need not fear those moments of being secret "lepers" ourselves, those parts of our being we hide away and lock up: our failures and sins, our vanities and deceptions, our jealousies and fakery. He will reach out to touch us there. It is only our denial that prevents the cure.

The gospel is also an invitation for us to enter into the being of Christ himself. If he is indeed our way, our truth, our life, then we make his person our own. We too can heal. We need not fear the visibly wounded who only remind us of our human frailty. The excluded and marginal, the ostracized and hidden, await our own touch. The very old or very ill need not threaten us if we allow them to name the truth of our shared inability to stand invulnerable before the world.

All of us are old. And all of us are frail. All of us, indeed, are handicapped. It's just that some of us can pretend better than others.

The prayer of the gospel's leper becomes our own when we finally realize that our afflictions—the interior even more than the visible—are not so much to be hidden and repressed as they are to be transformed. And then, one day, as we approach the table wherefrom Jesus himself becomes our food, becomes our very bodies, the prayers we have been saying for years might suddenly come more alive for us.

"Lord, I am not worthy to receive you, but only say the word and I shall be healed."

The communion of Eucharist is not only the sacrament whereby our bodies are transformed. It is also his response: "Of course I want to heal you."

13. The Paralysis of Unforgiven Guilt

Is. 43:18–25; 2 Cor. 1:18–22; Mk. 2:1–12

"It is I who wipe out your offenses."

When a good friend of mine died in her forties, an unfamiliar face appeared at the funeral and uttered a statement that almost floored me. "She must have had a lot of anger."

I don't know where his amateur psychology or spirituality came from, but I felt one of those rare impulses to punch someone in the nose. He may have uncovered an anger in me, but I thought he was totally wrong in his estimate of the woman we were mourning.

He was getting at something that seems fashionable in some circles: a contention that physical sickness is actually an expression of a spiritual or emotional illness. In its extreme forms this approach holds that every illness should be cured if faith is strong enough or, worse, that every organic illness is a symptom of a spiritual wound that must be healed.

Although there is an obvious integration and cross-relationship between our spiritual and physical states, I think that a simplistic equation of the two is hogwash. Does unhealed anger necessarily lead to cancer? Then may we suppose that Hitler, not a cancer sufferer, had a serene interior life? Or must we conclude that Jesus, when he drove the money-changers from the temple, was developing a malignancy?

What shall we say of moral monsters who are the picture of health? Or gentle souls racked with unbearable pain?

There is no easy answer to this. Since we humans are such complicated unities, our lives cannot be reduced to a tidy principle. The spiritual is not just some organic process going on in us. Nor is our physical condition merely a mirror of our faith life.

The psychic, spiritual, and physical are a dynamic unity in human persons. A sadness or unresolved tension may help induce an ulcer, which, in turn, may present us with a spiritual challenge. But there is no strict line that dictates their mutual effect. An identical habit of asceticism or spiritual discipline might enhance physical health or damage it. The same pattern of self-indulgence might seriously damage one person and not register at all on someone else. The fact that one gets sick and the other never sees a hospital room need not be a function of hidden angers or unresolved guilt.

Some of us do not take seriously enough the fact that we are organic bodies. We may think that mental illness, for example, is a matter of spiritual or emotional weakness and resist any suggestion that something might be wrong with neurons firing in our brains. We might be outraged at the recommendation that we could be helped by medicine.

Others don't take seriously the fact that we are embodied *spirits*—with the power to be aware of our own consciousness in relationship to our bodies and the world we inhabit. We can transcend our physical limits and wounds by the attitudes we take toward them. The clinical neurologist Oliver Sacks has confirmed this in his accounts of spiritual struggle waged by men and women stricken with the gravest of disabilities.

The dynamic unity of word and flesh, of body and spirit, is at the heart of Christian faith. We believe we can find the great and good transcendent God even in the most humble elements of the earth, like wheat and wine, even in the humblest humans, like a newborn child or a near-dying man on a cross.

When Christ at Capernaum healed a paralyzed man, he said, "Your sins are forgiven." He was not claiming that sins were the problem—certainly not the only problem—although sin can indeed paralyze us. He was telling us that spiritual cure is as crucial as physical cure.

Reports of healing dazzle us. They can bolster our faith. But forgiveness is just as resplendent. Isaiah knew that to be forgiven was as liberating as a rescue from the desert, as life-giving as water in a wasteland. For Jesus, the forgiveness he gave dissolved paralysis. He knew that, in more ways than one, we long to be whole again.

14. The New Law

Hos. 2:16–17, 21–22; 2 Cor. 3:1–6; Mk. 2:18–22

"No one pours new wine into old wineskins."

It is puzzling how some Christians turn to the Hebrew scripture, what many call the "old" testament, when they have trouble reconciling themselves with the "new." This can be an especially deft maneuver when one wants to find justification for certain practices which might not find approval in the Gospels or the various Epistles. Slaveowners, nationalists, proponents of capital punishment, and fervent militarists seem to find solace in the old wineskins of the Hebrew scripture—without, of course, subjecting themselves to the strictures of the law or the chastisement of the prophets, as a devout Jew assuredly does.

The law and prophets embody a powerful, authentic spirituality when received and lived as an organic whole. But when Christians select only part of it to justify behaviors incompatible with Christ's teachings, bad things can happen. Witness, for example, the treatment Christians have given their Jewish brothers and sisters in the past.

I do not mean by this that the God of Hosea is not the God of Jesus or his church. Hosea reveals for us Christians the promise of Christ, the marriage of eternal Word and human flesh. "I will espouse you to me forever: I will espouse you in right and in justice, in love and in mercy: I will espouse you in fidelity, and you shall know the Lord."

Morever, the law, in all its brilliance, reveals for us the will of God, which we find most fully present in Jesus. But the law is not the way of salvation. Jesus, who is our Law, is. And it is his Spirit, not the law, which gives our faith its life.

A particular example of an unhealthy mix of old and new is the Christian justification for capital punishment. The overwhelming message of the gospels makes it difficult to imagine Jesus recommending that we kill criminals or any other enemy. How can we possibly combine execution with "turning the other cheek," "not returning evil for evil," forgiving "seventy times seven," and Jesus' own identification with the least person imprisoned?

When Christians want to justify capital punishment, they assiduously avoid examining this "new wineskin" of Christ. They would rather pour the wine of their Christianity into an ancient skin which is not even theirs. And so they construct their arguments with citations from their "old" testament.

For authentic Christians, however, while the old law is honored, the "new" testament is precisely that: new.

When people complained to Jesus that his disciples did not fast as John's disciples and the Pharisees did, he reminded them of a homespun truth.

"Do not sew unshrunken cloth on an old cloak. If you do, the very thing you use to cover the hole pulls away, the new from the old, and the tear gets worse."

The followers of Moses and the prophets have their own charism and integrity. We Christians, however, will lose ours if we fail to see that Moses and the prophets have no life or value for us if our Lord has not come and saved us. He is the new, the whole fabric of our lives and labors. To attach our moral choices onto some older cloth will only sunder the integrity of the old as well as the new.

15. The Craft of Pharisees

Dt. 5: 12–15; 2 Cor. 4:6–11; Mk. 2:23–28

"Keep holy the Sabbath."

Who are the Pharisees of today? How do they approach religion? What is their manner in dealing with God's will?

The Pharisees of Mark's Gospel protested that Jesus' disciples, in gathering grain to eat, were doing things not permitted on the Sabbath. Jesus reminded them of the fact that King David himself, with his hungry men, ate the holy bread which was reserved only for priests. The point he eventually made was that the Sabbath was made for humans, not humans for the Sabbath. As if this were not enough, at the very moment when the Pharisees were hoping to bring an accusation against him, Jesus violated another Sabbath law, at least as they saw it, by healing a man's shriveled hand.

These questions of the law were no small matter to either side. Jesus became "deeply grieved that they had closed their minds against him." As for the Pharisees, after the disagreement, they began plotting with the Herodians to destroy him.

In this particular encounter we find a troubling disposition in the pharisaical mind: it is an inversion of the relationship between religion and God. Somehow the practices or tenets of religion come between the believer and the One believed in. Religion and its professionals, rather than being servants of God and humanity, become obstacles. Thus, the liberating intent of the Sabbath—fostering godly relationships and reminding men and women of their condition as loved creatures—is conscripted and confined into the service of the institution and its managers. The outer shell of the act is more important than the internal reality. The mediators of religion become more important than the God and the people they mediate.

Rather than entertain the image of the Pharisee as a curiosity from the distant past, perhaps we should ask whether we contemporary Christians face our own forms of pharisaism. Do we clerics sometimes mistake our roles? Is it priestcraft we practice, or ministry and service? Is it shepherding the flock or feathering our nests that we are about? Are we the indispensable ones in this thing called faith, or is it Someone other we can only point to?

Perhaps all Christians at some time or another fall into the trap of believing that our community, our laws, our traditions, our structures, even our sacraments are more important than the Incarnation itself. The signs of our redemption can loom larger than the actual victory Christ has won for us.

Paul reminds us that the truth we bear is something far more splendid than any bearer. "This treasure we possess in earthen vessels to make it clear that its surpassing power comes from God and not from us." Believers, priests, churches, all know afflictions and failure. But they need never be crushed, destroyed, or abandoned, because *what* is believed is always more important than the way it is formulated or defended.

If we fail to see this proper order of faith's life, that all our endeavors—even as church—are only earthen vessels, we may sadly find ourselves at the sorry state that some Pharisees themselves reached.

Finding it so intolerable that there was a greater authority than their own, they conspired with earthly powers to destroy the Lord and the liberty he brought.

16. The Great Refusal

Gn. 3:9–15; 2 Cor. 4:13–5:1; Mk. 3:20–35

"Sin against the Spirit."

Often over the years I have been asked how there might be a sin which could never be forgiven. The occasion for the question was invariably the incident in Mark's Gospel where scribes from Jerusalem charged that Jesus was possessed by Beelzebul, expelling demons by the power of the prince of demons.

Jesus defends himself, saying that a "house divided against itself cannot stand." Satan could never expel Satan unless he were to overthrow himself. Jesus, however, seems particularly incensed that people are so hardened in their resistance to him that they would claim he is possessed by the same unclean spirits he casts out. And this is what precipitates his harrowing assertion:

"I give you my word, every sin will be forgiven mankind and all the blasphemies men utter, but whoever blasphemes against the Holy Spirit will never be forgiven. He carries the guilt of his sin without end."

What is blasphemy against the Spirit? Why is it so devastating? How is it that such a sin could be so intractable before the will of God and the healing love of Christ?

Well, it is generally agreed that in the context of Mark's Gospel, this particular sin is the act of attributing the Holy Spirit's work in Jesus to the power of the devil. Thus, goodness itself is construed as evil. Some commentators add that there is a willful, persistent blindness which cynically interprets all good as trash.

No matter the variety of interpretations, one thing seems quite clear. This blasphemy against the Spirit is a radical resistance to grace and redemption. The outright rejection of Jesus' healing mission is unforgivable—not because God hates this sin particularly, but because this sin against the Spirit is a recalcitrant refusal to accept forgiveness. More impenetrable still, it sees every good as a masked evil.

This is the ultimately corrosive logic of deception that first raised its head in the Garden of Eden. All the goods of the earth were made to look tarnished by the deceptions of the serpent. The only imposter presented as the most desirable good was the rejection of God's will in denying our creatureliness.

The rejection of truth and the clinging to the deception, which characterized the sin of Adam and Eve, haunts every sin we enact. Yet all sins, even murder, unchastity, and apostasy, can be forgiven. What cannot be forgiven is the refusal to be forgiven, because the forgiveness, the grace of the Spirit offered, is mocked as evil.

The sin against the Spirit occurs when I say, "I refuse to acknowledge that I need forgiveness." I refuse to be forgiven. I refuse to believe that God has answered. I refuse to believe even that there is good, for it is only another face of the evil I believe in. "He casts out Satan by the power of Satan."

My own reflection on the unforgivable sin is this: I believe that if hell has a population it is peopled by those who have blasphemed against the Spirit. The weight of guilt without end is the weight of a lost soul burdened by the bitter thought that nothing is incarnate but evil and death. It is a weight that can be shared only by one who, in the words of Milton's awful antihero, could say, "Evil, be thou my good."

17. Floods and Deserts

Gen. 9:8–15; 1 Pet. 3:18–22; Mk. 1:1–15

"This is the time."

Death by water. Or death for lack of it. Whichever, they may well symbolize our deepest dreads.

The biblical story of the Great Flood, with its harrowing destruction, is generally believed to include early Mesopotamian accounts of wide disaster. But the Hebrew and Christian traditions interpret it in the context of history made intelligible by God. It has moral and spiritual import, not only for the people but for the person.

Floods strip us of everything, even the land to stand on. We can only wait or go under. If we sink, we suffocate. We disappear. Water is one of those great impersonal forces of the earth, before which we, even in our technological abundance, can find ourselves abandoned and helpless.

And yet water, despite its chaos, is the promise of life. Water is sustenance and cleansing. It is refreshment, purification, and promise. Thus Noah, as the embodiment of Israel, the church and perhaps all humankind, is given a regenerating covenant in the midst of utter loss. "There shall not be another flood to devastate the earth." Later, Isaiah (Ch. 54) will remind Israel of God's eternal love and pity—the only anchor in existence for Noah and all of us to depend on.

Jesus, too, knew the flood, the waters of death and life. And his going under in baptism became the first sign of his own death, his own passing through the chaos, his new covenant. His people would come to see the church, born of the water from his side, as the realization of Noah's promise.

The desert is also an image of lostness, if not death. It has its own chaos and dislocation. Dreadful and waterless, the desert can only be survived if it is traversed. To stop is to succumb.

And so, just as the Hebrew people spend forty reluctant years learning of the desert's hardship and wisdom, learning that only God can be their security and guide, learning that God alone can be their final food and water, so Jesus spends forty days in the desert of radical dependency, his bread not the result of his own power but of his feeding on the will of the One who sent him. He in turn will become our food, not only multiplying loaves in the desert, but offering his body as our nurture and drink.

Lent has a long history. By the end of the fourth century, its duration had fairly well been settled as the days between Quadragesima Monday and Holy Thursday. Eventually it was launched with the observance of Ash Wednesday, so that Jesus' own forty days in the desert could be re-enacted in Christian practice.

Earliest liturgical celebrations in Lent were framed in the context of baptism and penitence. We plunge into the covenant of Jesus and ratify our own symbolic admission of frailty before the forces of nature. By the tenth century, ashes became a dash of death's remembrance.

What pulls this all together is the bleak fate of death. We return to the dust from which we came, a terrible sentence. Capital punishment for us all: the fruit of sin, the rejection of our creatureliness, the refusal to be limited, even though loved.

For many, death makes life a cruel joke. Simone de Beauvoir said as much in *Force of Circumstance,* her bittersweet memoir of hopes, projects, and loves doomed to extinction. Bertrand Russell, in his own weighty autobiography, said that the entire sweep of human aspiration and accomplishment was little more than a dust heap before the laws of entropy.

What is the journey for? What is the upshot of this long trek through the deserts and barrenness, a few oases notwithstanding? Why wait, unmoored and tossed about on the sea of history?

It is not only humanity's destiny that prompts these questions. It is our own, yours and mine. Every death, if we are up to admitting it, is a catastrophe. We all go under. We all die dry and alone. Death is the flood unending, a wasteland that does not cease. Whether it is all water or all desert, life is a sheer irrational terror if water or desert is all there is.

And yet Lent invites us to enter the water and to walk the desert—to stare death itself in the face. Lent focuses on the two dominant symbols of our terror and asks us to pass through them to the other side.

God incarnate invites us. Jesus calls us to enter the waters of death with him, so as to rise. He leads us through the desert of godforsakenness to arrive at the land of promise. Lent is about our destiny.

Having not sinned himself, Jesus (Paul reminds us) became our sin and tasted its fruit of death in order to disarm it. As the "promised one," the promise of God, he also transforms the great images of dread to signs of life.

Christ is water that does not drown us but slakes our thirst and cleanses our sin. And he himself walks all the deserts of our lives to be the path through exile and serve as food and drink along the way.

Second Sunday of Lent

18. Being Put to the Test

Gen. 22:1–2, 9, 10–13, 15–18; Rom. 8:31–34;
Mk. 9:2–10

"This is my beloved."

The "test" of Abraham tests us all. It is a story that strains any confidence we might have in a loving God. Why would a good and gracious God order Abraham to sacrifice Isaac, "your only one, whom you love," the miracle child, the promise, the cherished gift?

Of course, Abraham is spared from carrying out the act by a heavenly angel of the Lord. But that doesn't make the plot any less troubling. It seems almost perverse that God would play such games with us.

Among the philosophers and theologians who have struggled with the story, Kierkegaard has been something of a beacon for me—even if not entirely illuminating. He reminds us of the utter transcendence and otherness of God, the absolute who enters our life not through rational categories or moral standards, but through a harrowing leap of faith. No wonder the imagery of dread, fear, and trembling haunted Kierkegaard's mind.

It was another philosopher, however, who opened up new possibilities for me. Professor Eleonore Stump, who holds the Henle Chair in Philosophy at Saint Louis University, has been making innovative forays into scriptural narrative. She is as much at home with the contemporary mind-body problem as she is with medieval thought, and when she accompanies the likes of Aquinas it is at the intersection of philosophy and theology. In a recent lecture she examined the story of Abraham.

Stump situates the sacrifice of Isaac in the context of Sarah, Hagar, and Ishmael. Sarai, in her seventies, we may recall, had borne no child for Abraham. She then offered Hagar, her Egyptian maidservant, to Abraham as his wife. Hagar gave birth to Ishmael, a source of joy to Abraham at the ripe age of eighty-six, but an irritating source of jealousy and resentment to Sarai.

Thirteen years later, God, while ensuring a fruitful and happy fate for Hagar's Ishmael, offers a new covenant to Abraham, with the promise of a son for Sarai, now to be called Sarah, at the age of ninety.

At the time of Isaac's weaning, however, Sarah's jealousy gets the better of her, and she insists that Abraham cast Hagar and Ishmael out into the wilderness. Abraham is pained, but he easily accepts God's reassurance that both will survive. Giving them some bread and a skin of water, he casts them out.

Now Stump points out the ambivalence of Abraham's abandoning his dear son Ishmael to the wilds with little to protect or sustain him. True, Abraham was following God's will, but with no resistance, confident of the happy result that Sarah would be placated. And the expulsion of Hagar and Ishmael could be nothing less than a terrible betrayal of trust, even if mitigated by the presumption that Abraham informed them of God's promise.

Years later, when Isaac reaches the same age Ishmael had been when he was banished, the ambivalence would be removed.

In words and context much the same as those of the Ishmael incident, we read that Abraham is once again in the situation of dispatching the son he loves. This time, however, there are no beneficial side effects that might alleviate his pain. All Abraham has is his trust that God is good and will keep his promises.

The whole point of the episode is to test whether Abraham believes that God is trustworthy. The issue is Abraham's state of mind: if he truly believes the word of God, then he knows with utter conviction that "God will provide." His readiness to sacrifice Isaac is neither moral compromise nor endangerment to his son—if he indeed believes that Isaac is God's promise of future generations. In faith, Abraham knows, "Even if he die, he shall live."

Well, we know that Isaac died, but not by the hand of Abraham. It was by the exigence of earthly existence. And yet Isaac fathered generations of grace and abundance.

I cannot be sure of the full accuracy of my account of Professor Stump's reflections, but I left her lecture with a new appreciation of Abraham's test. If I believe that God is good and will keep his promises, the test is not as cruel or irrational as I first thought. What is more, I think this story concerns more than Isaac's death. It is about the death of us all.

Each of us is required to make Abraham's sacrifice. We all must face the inevitability of letting go our most beloved person, task, accomplishment, joy. Everything dear to us, everything given to us by God is subject to death: its own and our own.

The essence of the story is this: Is God good? And will God keep his promises? Abraham is our father in faith because he embodies the final act of faith that all of us must make. We all face the sacrifice. We all stand before the terrible relinquishment of everything we hold most dear.

And our very God does the same. "This is my beloved Son." God's "only begotten," one of our own kind, will go through our passages—even the passage of death.

God has made the promise not only to Abraham and to us. God has made the promise to God's very self.

"Is it possible that God, who did not spare his only Son but handed him over for the sake of us all, will not grant us all things besides?"

19. Imperatives of Faith

Ex. 20:1–17; 1 Cor. 1:22–25; Jn. 2:13–25

"Keep my commandments."

"I, the Lord, am your God, who brought you out of the land of Egypt, that place of slavery. You shall not have other gods besides me. You shall not carve idols for yourselves in the shape of anything. . . ."

If you think about it, the commandments seem almost a strange, outmoded language. One of my ethics students, in fact, somewhat facetiously, numbered among his revised "commandments for America": "Thou shalt not commit adultery without a condom."

We are a people given to exceptions and excuses. Context, individuality, personal choice, and private fulfillments dominate our moral discourse. Philosophically speaking, we are a nation of utilitarians and libertarians. It is no wonder, then, that commandments that seem to disregard our pleasure and instead offer us imperatives seem cranky.

We bridle at limits. Especially moral limits. Our talk complains of guilt trips and warns us against the tyranny of shoulds. But, as is often the case, we caution ourselves against the sins we are least likely to commit. Our problem is not that we are a guilt-ridden and scrupulous people. We are not self-denying ascetics. We are not crimped by moral confinement. It's just the opposite.

We resist limits. We bristle at anything that might hold us responsible or duty-bound. This not only means trouble for those around us, whether nations or neighbors. It also means trouble for God. People or countries who delude themselves into thinking they have no limits soon start thinking they are gods themselves.

But the United States was not the first, nor does it remain the only, example of moral exceptionalism. Christianity itself can be seen as a history of making exceptions to God's law. One would fall in exhaustion trying to count the exceptions Christians have made to killing: not just the most familiar excuses of self-defense and national security, but revenge, class, racism, inconvenience, religious intolerance, money, and "to insure our way of life." And that's just one of the commandments.

We're uncomfortable with all of them. We're uncomfortable with law, with duties, with responsibility.

Admittedly, these concepts can represent an intolerable burden; but some of us seem incapable of any appreciation of any law we ourselves have not cooked up. My philosophy students in ethics are at first appalled by the moral vision of Immanuel Kant, with its insistence on the ethical excellence of duty. For Kant, indeed, the only grounds for any moral approbation of a human act was the fact that it was done for duty's sake and not merely according to duty. He held that our happiness had little or nothing at all to do with moral dignity. This is sheer heresy for our cultural consciousness. And yet, when you reflect upon Kant's observations, he makes a striking case for the nobility of following a moral command for the sake of duty.

Who is more morally sublime, Kant would ask us: the spouse who is faithful because he is happy and fulfilled or because—even in the midst of difficulties and hardship—he is true to his duty? Who is truly moral: the woman who stays alive because she enjoys living or the one who continues to live even in pain and sorrow because it is her duty to honor the gift God has given her?

God does not advise us not to kill. God commands us. And it is a command not based upon whether we are happy or productive, or whether we are dealing with our friends, coreligionists, good Americans, or the innocent. Yet we all make exceptions: the ancient Jewish people as well as the contemporary Jewish state, medieval Christians as well as modern Catholics, Kant as well as Aquinas. History serves, Hegel said, as little more than a slaughtering block.

There is more than one paradox in all of this. Each of the commandments, it can be said, is not some external and irrational fiat from an alien God. Rather, each is an expression of the truth God has made in us. If we worship idols or worship our work, if we covet person or property, if we dishonor those who have given us life, we not only reject the law of God, we destroy what we are. For the duty imposed on us by God is not a function of Kant's pure rationality or some arbitrary legislation of a distant deity. It is the duty to be true to what we are—limited but loved creatures.

Jesus, for Christians, is the new law, the law of God enfleshed. He is not only "truly God," our creed says; he is "truly human." His life, like the commandments themselves, may be a stumbling block and an absurdity to us at times, but we proclaim it, nonetheless, our way and our truth. The commandments, all encompassed in the new commandment of love of God and neighbor, may seem folly, but God's folly is wiser than human provision.

We will always struggle with this. And since Jesus himself has promised to remain in our midst, we can look to him as a healing of our guilt.

But we should be forewarned. He may come to us with words as stern as those he spoke to the people despoiling the temple. "You have turned it into a den of thieves."

20. Being Saved by God's Kind Favor

2 Chr. 35:14–17, 19–23; Eph. 2:4–10; Jn. 3:14–21

"This is not your own doing. It is God's gift."

When I was a preteen, I used to be embarrassed by those signs, some of them in garish neon, which sported the phrase, "Jesus Saves." It seemed so primitive. I also remember those Sunday morning television programs that piously ended with, "I have come that they may have life and have it more abundantly." Who on earth would be so arrogant as to make such a claim? And I also thought for the longest time that the "IHS" over graves stood for "I have suffered," a somewhat self-indulgent epitaph. Little did I know that "IHS" means Jesus.

It has all changed for me—as, I think, it does for any believer who persists in the journey, who lives through disappointments and disillusionments, who comes to the startling realization that there is no way under the sun for us to save ourselves.

Our sacraments, our rituals, our prayers, and popes mean little if Christ has not saved us, if Jesus has not given us the promise of abundant life, if he has not, indeed, suffered and died for us.

One day in this journey of faith, I was reminded how easily we misunderstand and are misunderstood in these matters of belief. While teaching a seminar on the philosophy of Sigmund Freud, I was confronted by a Christian fundamentalist graduate student one evening after class.

"I think you Catholic priests were misled in your training."

For some reason, my hunch was that he was upset by my friendly but critical reading of Freud. I defended myself: "We can all learn a lot from nonbelievers."

"I don't mean Freud," he said. "It's your seminary training that has led you away from the truth."

In retrospect, I don't know what prompted me next to say what I did, but with a tone of resignation I sighed: "I can't remember much of what I learned in four years of theology, but not much of my faith rides on it. All I know is that my life would be meaningless if Christ has not saved us."

His jaw dropped. "You actually believe that Christ has saved you."

"Of course. Otherwise, I'd have no hope."

"But you Catholics believe that priests and rituals save you. You think the pope and Mary save you."

"No, those things are great, but they're a waste of time if Christ hasn't saved us."

He couldn't believe it. I guess he thought I was still the child embarrassed by the "Jesus Saves" sign. It was no longer an embarrassment. It was my hope.

The people of Judah had to have a similar hope. They surely could not trust in their own righteousness. Their priests and people only piled up infidelities. They amassed abominations. They mocked and scoffed. Only a good and gracious God could have compassion, overcome their infidelities, and lead them back from exile. "God so loved the world," Jesus told Nicodemus, the seeker by night, "as to give his only Son."

This is not as easy to accept as it first may seem. To be loved as a free gift, to be saved by the favor of another is a precarious state of affairs.

Paul, in a splendid passage from Ephesians, is well aware of our reluctance to entrust ourselves to God's love. That is why he seems compelled to reiterate: "I repeat, it is owing to God's favor that salvation is yours through faith. This is not your own doing. It is God's gift. Neither is it a reward for anything you have accomplished."

"Oh, if it could only be our accomplishment," we might say in high and happy times. We would love to point to our successes, our virtues and improvements, our earnestness in trying so hard, our ardent confessions or even our nine first Fridays. But it is not our own doing, this salvation. It is not a result of our effort.

On the other hand, in our times of failure or discouragement we may lament, "Alas, we have accomplished nothing." If only we could have made ourselves more worthy, if only we had tried harder, if only we had succeeded in our task of self-perfection.

Again, we sadly miss the point. We stumble about in the dark, bereft of the hope that we had in our projects, stripped of plans that might have saved us, purged of the pretense that we had no need of redemption. We are unaware that, when we acknowledge the futility of our efforts, we are at the moment of conversion. It is the very invitation to abandonment to divine grace.

True, we can resist the hope, we can hate the light, we can fear the exposure to love and to the truth on which it rests. And our resistance can come between us and the love of God revealed in Jesus Christ. We can refuse to accept the grace that is always there.

As men and women of faith, our major labor and effort is not to achieve our salvation. It is to entrust ourselves to it. "God is rich in mercy; because of his great love for us he brought us to life with Christ when we were dead in sin. By this favor you were saved."

21. Repentance and Eucharist

Jer. 31:31–34; Heb. 5:7–9; Jn. 12:20–33

"I will remember their sin no more."

A number of years ago I was starting an eight-day retreat with more than ordinary reluctance. Retreats had often carried a sense of foreboding for me, a journey into truth that might just as well be postponed or avoided. The solitude and prayer would make me face myself in ways not always pleasant.

I felt particularly unprepared. I don't think I had prayed for a continuous hour over the previous months. I had been neglecting the prayer of the church in the priest's "office." My work with the sacraments seemed good enough, but I had the distinct feeling that I was doing it all for myself. I was resentful of people who asked for my help, jealous of my time, and ashamed of my self-centeredness.

The retreat director said: "Great. You're just where you should be when you enter the presence of God." His advice seemed like some of that "don't worry, be happy" stuff, and I told him as much.

"Well, how does every Mass begin?" he asked.

"In the name of the Father. . . ."

"No, what is the first formal part of the Eucharist?"

And then it came to me: the penitential rite. "Lord, have mercy." He had reminded me that the acknowledgment of sin was the condition for entry into the covenant of the Eucharist.

What is more, I've come to see that the admission of sin is a constant theme of every Mass. I do not mean the implicit willingness to "repent and believe the Good News" when we hear the word of God, or the acknowledgment of our inadequacy when we offer our prayers of the faithful. I mean, rather, the continuing acknowledgment of our sinful condition at the height of the Communion rite.

In the Our Father, we pray that God "forgive us our sins as we forgive those who have sinned against us"—a scary proposal, if you spend a minute thinking about it.

Whether we forgive or not, however, the presumption that we are sinners is painfully evident. It's inescapable. The celebrant asks God, "Look not upon our sins, but on the faith of your church," immediately prior to the exchange of peace. It is a sinful church that chants: "You who take away the sins of the world, have mercy on us." It is the church's priest who prays before Communion: "By your holy body and blood, free me from all my sins."

The lifted-up body and blood of Christ—drawing all things to himself—"takes away the sins of the world." Our response is to confess that, although we are not worthy, we are healed at the word of God.

The acknowledgment of our sin is not an embarrassing hindrance to God's presence. It is the prompting of God's law, Jeremiah reminds us, written in our hearts. It is the condition of the new covenant itself. It is the reason for Jesus' covenant. "This is the cup of my blood, the blood of the new and everlasting covenant. It will be shed for you and for all so that sins may be forgiven."

There are many things we take seriously about our worship —the setting, the music, the preaching—but I wonder if we take seriously enough its very ritual words and their meaning. The Consecration is actually incomprehensible if we think we are sinless. After all, it is the re-enactment of Christ's sacrifice for the forgiveness of our sins.

Our admission of sin is the occasion for singing the glories of God. It is the appreciation of how happy we are to be called to the supper. It is the acceptance of the new covenant, Christ's passion and death embodied in our Eucharist. When we take Communion, we take the new law, the new covenant, literally into our bodies, our hearts. And the promise of

Jeremiah is realized in the flesh: "I am yours and you are mine. I will remember your sin no more." It is as important to remember why Christ died for us as it is to remember that he did so. In fact, the paschal mystery, as well as the Eucharist, cannot make very much sense at all if we fail to understand how much we need both. "You have set us free, you are the Savior of the world."

It is impossible to enter the presence of God, whether in a retreat or in a liturgy, as self-made men and women. We cannot enter the covenant blameless and spotless. Nor can we rely upon our good works to make us worthy of this covenant. The only contribution we make to this covenant is the acknowledgment of our sin and the trust that it is healed by the redemptive power of God's love.

If our experience of the Eucharist is bland or boring, if our liturgies seem lifeless or contrived, could it be at least in part due to the fact that we do not take seriously either our sinfulness or God's forgiveness?

After all, the words "I will remember their sin no more" are not very liberating or exciting if people think they have no sins to remember.

22. Dying

Is. 50:4–7; Phil. 2:6–11; Mk. 14:1–15:47

"My heart is filled with sorrow to the point of death."

I can admit now that when I was young, I hated those movies portraying the life of Christ. They were never snazzy enough. The miracles were never convincing. To top it off, those movies always ended in failure. There is no way around it. He died. He failed. And it was a mess.

Perhaps that is why I rarely found our churches very appealing. In addition to the associations of glumness and guilt, there he was, bleeding and broken up, for all to see.

One of the best things about the Forty Hours devotion was the fact that, in addition to the incense and the processions, the cross, especially the body, would soon be covered.

Much later in life I would hear reports that the Reverend Sun Myung Moon, the head of the Unification Church, as well as Ted Turner, found it somewhat strange that people would worship a figure who ended up in such failure.

And that's what it was all about. I wanted, we all want, a winner. And a winner does not end up like the rest of us— weak, beyond earthly help, frail, and failing before the great force of death.

Superman had X-ray eyes and could fly. Captain Marvel muttered "Shazam!" and zapped defeat into sudden victory. Wonder Woman, better than the Amazons, could take on armies of marauders. But not Jesus.

I would have rewritten the script. Instead of picking up the ear of an enemy and somehow reattaching it, why not have Jesus use that power to knock all their heads off?

Even after Jesus was put on the cross, I thought the cavalry could have come in at the last minute. The heavens could have opened up and the thunderous voice of God boom: "What are you doing to my beloved Son? Take that!" Lightning and earthquakes. Instead we get this: "My God, my God, why have you forsaken me?"

I chose then to ignore this unpleasantness for years. Easter would come sure enough, candy, spring, and all.

This avoidance reappeared when I became a Jesuit novice. I could never adequately enter the mystery of the third week of the Spiritual Exercises, the week (or day, as the case may be) that concentrated on the passion and death of Jesus. Everything seemed to come to a stop. I would wait for the resurrection narratives and the promise of the retreat's end.

Somehow, over the years, it has all changed. A child knows death but not its implications. Most adults do.

When you get right down to it, every death is disaster. Death is a total, utter negation of everything that leads up to it. Many nonbelievers, in their more honest moments, admit the unmentionable: death seems to mock our every hope and achievement.

And after seeing so many loved ones die, whether old and frail, middle-aged and struck down by infirmity, young and suddenly disappeared, I realize that nothing less than a God who would face our death could suffice.

Could a God truly love and heal us, all so burdened with sin and its weight of death, if that God, too, had not been filled somehow with sorrow, even to the point of death?

Easter Sunday

23. Rising

Acts 10:34, 37–43; Col. 3:1–4; Jn. 20:1–9

"Be intent on things above rather than things of earth."

The postmodern world has problems with resurrection. It has problems with anything transcendent. This life is all there is. You only go around once. Grab all the gusto. It doesn't get any better than this. Bound by immediate distraction, enthralled by skills of indulgence, we are jarred by talk of heaven. It is inappropriate.

Discomfort with transcendence churns in us Christians as well. We want to make good sense of our faith, especially to those who think our beliefs a bit outdated. Our own discourse becomes less a matter of heaven and hell, forgiveness and redemption, than of self-fulfillment, illness and recovery, and how to be our own best friends. Sometimes there even seems to be a hidden assumption lurking in our theology and ritual: This life is all there is. And—although more rarely—complaints can still be heard from premodern survivors that they rarely hear homilies and sermons about the four last things.

We are very much a people of this age, the here and now. But to the extent that we partake of postmodern sensibility, we are on a collision course with the content of our worship. In fact, if we ever thought for a minute about the reality we claim is taking place in our Eucharists, we might run for cover.

Or cover it up. Do we speak much to each other about the fact that there is something much more astounding than warm fellowship happening in our churches? Do we expend much energy over a sacramental reality that is more stirring than music and crafted homilies? Do we admit that the act of our liturgy is more significant than its style and decor?

The Eucharist is about our salvation and our destiny, or it is nothing. It is the pledge of eternal forgiveness. And Communion is not a mere bread for earthly flesh. Quite the contrary, it is nutrition for transformed bodies. It is the sustenance of wayfarers on their way beyond this life. It is the bread of angels, the food of heaven.

Easter is Eucharistic because it is the promise of an eternal banquet. Christ, having entered into the depths of our humanity, even to the extent of dying its death, is claimed as risen.

Of course there are people who say that this cannot have happened. It was projection, a fabrication, a corporate wish-fulfillment. But the accounts of his followers seem quite otherwise. Something most real had happened to them. They said that their master had appeared to them bodily.

It is their witness which is at the origins of our faith.

If we take soberly enough the passion and death of our own lives, of humanity itself, and of Jesus who is the eternal Word made flesh, we will more fully appreciate the radical nature of our faith, especially at Eastertime.

We believe there is more than meets the eye. There is more than the earth in all its might, more than our projects and exploits in all their splendor.

"We believe in the resurrection of the body and the life of the world to come."

Say "Amen," somebody.

24. Community Transformations

Acts 4:32–35; 1 Jn. 5:1–6; Jn. 20:19–31

"I'll never believe it."

We have a glowing picture of the early Christian community: one heart, one mind, no one of them claimed anything as his or her own. So stunning was their witness that respect was paid by all. There were no needy in their midst, and each was provided for according to need. Perhaps they felt, in the words recorded in the First Letter of John, that, as believers in Jesus as Son of God, they could take on the world.

The account of the earliest community, however—the community hidden behind locked doors, the community hiding in fear—reveals that perhaps not all was sweetness and light. It is noteworthy that the first word attributed to the risen Lord is "peace." One can presume, then, that this community was somehow in a state of disquiet. And it seems that the reason was not only fear and terrible disappointment. Quite possibly it may have been divisiveness, since it is forgiveness that Jesus next addresses: "If you forgive others' sins, they are forgiven them; if you hold them bound, they are held bound."

What is it that is to be forgiven by the gift of the Spirit's breath?

Scripture recounts that "it happened" that Thomas was absent when Jesus came. Later the community greets Thomas with the words, "We have seen the Lord." And he quite simply refuses to accept their testimony.

"I'll never believe it without probing the nail-prints in his hands, without putting my hand into his side."

Whether this was a major source of division or not, it is evident that Thomas is the first Christian to dissent formally from a fundamental conviction of the gathered church. After all, he does not believe in their testimony to the Resurrection.

Despite the wound of this division, however, Thomas remains with the community and they seem to welcome him. In fact, the next time Jesus appears in their midst, a week later, Thomas is present. And Jesus speaks directly to him: "Do not persist in your unbelief, but believe."

I have found this a fascinating and rather challenging narrative. Even if forgiveness is not the theme of the Thomas incident, it is clearly the case that Thomas is with the community he so profoundly challenges.

I'm afraid that if I had been running the church it might have been otherwise. I find in myself strong inclinations to exclude from the category of believers those who seem to reject significant parts of our doctrine and practice. And yet, the example of the resurrection community undermines such an attitude. Thomas was not excluded. He was not kicked out or given an either-or choice concerning the Resurrection of Christ. He was welcome. Apparently, he was forgiven, not bound, even though at the time he had not yet recanted his heresy.

I wonder what this might mean for a church that has strong tendencies to exclude the marginal.

Again, I am not constitutionally inclined to take much delight in such an observation, but the evidence of the text warrants it. And it says something important to us all. We have not a few liberals and conservatives who act as if the presence of the other side is a contaminant in the church. There have been wars and persecutions mounted in the name of dogma. There have been excommunications and interdicts in the name of right practice. Divisions have wounded the church and injured our witness in faith. The passion for being right has served the cause of ego at least as much as it has served the cause of Christ.

Does this mean that anything goes, that there is no cause or truth worth standing up for and making divisions over? Is it an invitation to the chaos of diversity without any center or unity? Not necessarily.

What provided the occasion for the renewed entry of Jesus into the community was the fact that they were gathered together in his name. At least Thomas had not hardened himself to their testimony. At least he had not put himself out of and above the church. He may have had the attitude of a dissenter, but it was in the context of Christ as the center of their relationship. There is division, but there is also humility and openness.

Jesus says to the Thomas in us: "Enter the wounds: the wounds of my humanity, of my church, of my crucified body, my risen body and my mystical body."

And the reply of Thomas, the doubter, the unbeliever, the skeptic? In the strongest divinity text of the New Testament, albeit a text probably appended later, he says, "My Lord and my God." Such is the transformative power of resurrection faith.

"These have been recorded to help you believe that Jesus is the Messiah, the Son of God, so that through this faith you may have life in his name."

May they help us believe. And forgive.

25. Glorified Bodies

Acts 3:13–15; 1 Jn. 2:1–5; Lk. 24:35–48

"A ghost does not have flesh and bones as I do."

Peter claims, in the Acts of the Apostles, that the servant Jesus has been glorified. Among other things, such a claim might be referring to the testimonies, recounting about the risen Lord, that the third Gospel drew upon.

While the disciples who had returned from the road to Emmaus were explaining how they recognized Jesus in the breaking of bread, Jesus suddenly appeared in their midst. Frightened, they thought they were seeing a ghost, but Jesus told them to look at his wounds and even touch him. He knew they were having trouble believing what was before them. As if to convince them that he was somehow, albeit strangely, flesh and blood, he asked for something to eat in their presence.

This, like other accounts of the risen Jesus, is amazingly wonderful. And despite the efforts of countless commentators and interpreters over the centuries to reduce these narratives to something neither quite so strange nor nearly so wonderful, one fact remains: The resurrection community that had experienced Jesus' dying now experienced his risen presence. And it was, quite insistently, an embodied one.

This is a Jesus of sight and sound, of memories and relationships, of love and tenderness. He would take food and allow himself to be touched. Even his wounds could be examined. It was a recognizable and identifiable Jesus, a realization of his bodied existence. And yet he seemed to transcend the conditions of sheer organic materiality. He would appear out of nowhere, supposedly pass through walls and closed doors, walk on water, and reveal wounds startlingly different from the open sores of earthly trauma.

Often enough, we have come across claims that this cannot be literally true. But what if it were true? Either this is all bunkum, or there is some kind of bodied existence that is not the same as our sheer physical limitedness. It is a kind of existence that enters our world yet is not cramped by it.

Human destiny after death appears to have fascinated every human community. In fact, some of our most ancient encounters with our forebears are through their artifacts that portray the transition of death. Earliest oral traditions, sagas, and myths speak of the journey beyond our body's door. Philosophers, even the early Greeks, seemed preoccupied with questions of immortality. Plato, not very friendly to the body in any case, thought that on some purely psychic or intellectual level we not only outlasted our bodies—we predated them too.

Many before Miguel Unamuno, of our own century, found this solution outrageous. After all, we are not just souls or psyches or minds. We—our identities, our selves—are living, breathing, embodied spirits, laced together with memories, sensations, commitments, gender, relationships, and intelligence.

Thomas Aquinas saw this problem as early as the thirteenth century. There is no way we could talk of personal immortality or our destiny if our bodies were not somehow part of the picture. If a disembodied soul survived our deaths, that might be nice, but it certainly would not be us. We are ensouled bodies. A separated soul may live on—but it would be drastically incomplete.

This is why Aquinas loved to dwell on the resurrection narratives. It suggested to him that we, like Jesus, would have a new bodied existence, truly related to our bodies in this world, but nonetheless freed from their organic disabilities. Thus he waxes eloquent in the *Summa Contra Gentiles* about the kind of bodies we might have in the next life: fully realized even if we died young, fully supple if we died old and frail, capable of every bodied joy, and gloriously transcendent of our every body-wound.

While the immortality of the soul was a proposition Aquinas held on the evidence of reason, the immortality of the body he affirmed on faith—faith in the Resurrection. We Christians believe in glorified bodies, resurrected bodies. These days we are receiving strange confirmations of such beliefs by the numerous accounts of near-death and out-of-body experiences. But our convictions go back to the testimony of our first brothers and sisters in faith, those who experienced Christ in his body, but so gloriously that even his wounds were lovely invitations to faith.

You can have your hunches about robbed tombs, Passover plots, mass hysteria, and orchestrated illusion. Paltry fare. As for me, Dante touches the mystery of the gospel witness as well as he does our own longing.

In Canto Fourteen of the *Paradiso,* the voice of Dante's Solomon sings of our bodies' destiny, embraced by heaven. Every promise of the body, the splendor of our organic life, shall be lustrous and strong. Nothing good of this wondrous world of sense and sentiment shall be lost. All will be gloriously preserved as Christ's own body was:

> "Long as shall last the feast of Paradise,
> Even so long," it said, "our love shall lace
> This radiance round us for our festal guise.
> . . .
> And when we put completeness on afresh,
> All the more gracious shall our person be,
> Reclothed in the holy and glorious flesh."

26. Other Sheep

Acts 4:8–12; 1 Jn. 3:1–2; Jn. 19:11–18

"There is no salvation in anyone else."

One of my earliest schoolday memories is concern for pagan babies. We would have collections or be given little banks for the purpose of saving them one at a time. There might even be pictures or names we could relate to, sent to us by missionaries.

Some of us wondered what happened to all the countless children of the world who suffered, not only for lack of food, but for want of faith in Jesus. Limbo was proposed as an answer to our cares. It wasn't heaven. But it was not hell. Small comfort for us would-be lawyers quarrelling over equity and fairness in the universe.

The problem was made worse by Bible history. All those heroes and heroines—Moses and Miriam, David and Ruth, Sarah and Noah—assigned to limbo? By high school I had uncomfortably added other names, from Socrates to Gandhi. And the sophistication of adulthood did not ease the irritation.

I eventually found myself team-teaching Dante's *Divine Comedy* with Professor Albert William Levi, a brilliant philosopher, dear friend, and agnostic Jew. Although he valued much of what Christ said and did, he was not a follower. He appreciated believers but did not share their faith.

When we came to the last cantos of the *Purgatorio* and found the "earthly paradise," my graduate students were upset that not only Virgil but Professor Levi as well could not pass into heaven. (Levi himself was not as concerned: "The earthly paradise is more than I might hope for, and what wonderful company with Plato, Homer, Cicero, and Virgil to boot!")

Limbo and the earthly paradise, like the notions "baptism of desire" and "baptism of blood," are all responses of Christian piety and imagination to the incongruous possibility of innocent millions unsaved by Christ.

Peter, after all, preaches in Acts that "there is no salvation in anyone else, for there is no other name in the whole world given to the human race by which we are to be saved." And we have all been given the word that "unless you are born of water and the spirit, you shall not enter" (Jn. 3:5).

But what is the "rebirth"? And how is it that Jesus is savior of the world? Must the power of his name be constrained by our own hearing of it? Are our sacraments, our words, and our teachings the required condition for salvation, or are they the signs of the salvation Jesus has already won for us?

The Christian faith itself is a sign of what God does in us, rather than something we create as a requirement to meet God. We must not confuse the ontological reality of God's providential love for us with the psychological reality of how we receive it.

Ontologically, there is no salvation outside of Christ. It is only by his being the Word made flesh, the Son of God, that we are all indeed made God's children. It is by the fact of God taking our body, dying our death, and rising in Jesus that our destinies are forever changed. God now looks upon all human flesh and sees the face of the beloved Son.

Psychologically, we may not know such a wondrous thing has happened to us. But the only way to resist this fact would be consciously to reject its possibility.

Today's Gospel has Jesus say, "I have other sheep that do not belong to this fold." Could this be applied to all those who are not Christians but are nonetheless open to the fullest reality of Christ? Could it be that the way he leads them and speaks to them is through the very movement of the human heart itself, which has now been reclaimed by the heart of the Word made flesh?

At the bottom of our being is a hope for some unconstricted good that meets the hunger of our will. It moves in rhythm with the passion of our minds, insatiable for truth. The question every human faces is whether such hope and passion is groundless.

As for us who have encountered Christ, we profess in faith that the answer has been spoken in the Word made flesh. For those who have not met Christ, the task is to be faithful to the question of their hearts and hope that an answer is given. Christ is that answer, whether they know it or not.

My friend Professor Levi told me that, as much as he would like it, he had not been given the gift of faith. But he had been given the gift of our humanity, lavishly so—one shared with and transformed by Jesus.

And so, before he died, I asked this man of fine mind and great longing two questions: "Are you open to all the truth there is to be known? Are you open to all the good there is to be loved?"

"Of course," he said. "How could I not be?"

That was enough to know that his heart would not stop at the earthly paradise. Not only was he a child of God. In his own way, he heard the voice of the Shepherd.

27. Radical Faith

Acts 9:26–31; 1 Jn. 3:18–24; Jn. 15:1–8

"I am the vine, you are the branches."

"Have you accepted Christ as your personal savior?" How do you respond to that question? Uneasily, if you are like me for much of my life. The question had seemed far too direct and intense. It also struck me as being a bit overdone on the emotional side. A little extreme.

"Personal savior" talk suggested the kind of display, seen in Billy Graham's crusades, that sometimes makes other Christians, especially Catholics, rather uncomfortable. "Come forward as a witness that you are claiming Christ as your redeemer." Then the long lines of men and women, coursing through the aisles like blood through arteries, drain down to the stage to make public their dependency on the Lord.

Lately it has become evident to me that such uneasiness is paradoxical. After all, Catholics are a people who have made a Sunday, if not a daily, ritual of leaving their pews, proceeding to the altar, and receiving the body and blood of Christ.

Perhaps we have gotten too familiar with it, but our sacramental Eucharist, our holy Communion, is a most radical, direct, and intense expression of the conviction that Christ is our personal savior. It is easy to overlook how extreme our dogma and ritual appear to others. Just look at the facts.

We have been so steadfast and insistent on the "real presence" in our traditions that this has often divided us from our brothers and sisters in faith who do not agree with the metaphysical category of transubstantiation. We cling to it because it is our way of saying that our Savior is most fully and truly found in the Eucharist.

Catholics believe that Jesus Christ, body and blood, soul and divinity, is really present under the appearances of bread and wine. We believe it is more than fellowship that we celebrate. It is more than commemoration and remembrance. Something far greater than our prayer and action is taking place.

We profess that we re-enact the saving mystery of the passion and death of Jesus, and this very mystery becomes our food. By receiving Communion we profess that Christ's saving of us is our sustenance. We could not live or survive without it.

If we believe in the real presence, what then do we actually think takes place in the Eucharist? We hold that the full reality of Jesus Christ enters our body. He is our food. He actually becomes part of us and we a part of him. We are thereby re-enacting the central story of our redemption: that the eternal Word would take human flesh and dwell among us. The One who sent the Word now looks upon us and sees within us the real presence of Jesus. Thereby we are saved. We, in turn, look upon each other, even the least, and see the face of Christ. Thereby we are sent.

Now that is intense. That is radical.

The reception of Communion makes no sense if we do not intend it to affirm that Christ is our personal savior. What could be more personal, more intense, than to say, "You are my food and drink, you are my own very flesh and blood"?

In our approach to the altar, our coming forward to receive the body and blood of Christ, we sacramentally embody Billy Graham's procession of witnesses. When we acknowledge that Christ is our way, truth, and life, our savior and redeemer, our sustenance, we are united not only with our fellow believers who do not share our communion, but also with Paul, so wholly given to the mystery of his ransom by Christ, and with the school of John, sustained by the belief that God is in them and Christ's Spirit is with them.

If the sacrament of Eucharist is not taken intensely, personally, and radically, it does not make much sense at all. But if we take it seriously, even our scripture takes on deeper meaning. In the fourth Gospel's account of the Last Supper, we find an ever-intensifying invitation by Jesus to root our lives totally in him. He seeks a full union with us, "so that where I am you may be too" (14:3). He promises us that we will live in him, and he will live in us, just as he lives in unity with the Father.

"I have given them the glory you gave to me, that they may be one as we are one. With me in them and you in me, may they be so completely one that the world will realize that it was you who sent me and that I have loved them as much as you loved me" (17:22–23). In the midst of this prayer for total identification with us, the image of the vine and branches is presented as an extended portrayal of our living in Christ for sustenance and fruitfulness.

"I am the vine, you are the branches. You who live in me, and I in you, will produce abundant fruit, for apart from me you can do nothing." This is not a tame claim. It is a bold assertion that we have no being, no life, apart from Christ. "Live on in me, as I do in you."

If you believe that, you believe that Christ is your personal savior.

28. Hankering after the "Old Faith"

Acts 10:25–26, 34–35, 44–48; 1 Jn. 4:7–10; Jn. 15:9–17

"This is my commandment: love one another."

The two men who came to visit were immaculately dressed. There was a sweetness about their courtesy, even though you could sense they were stern. They came to present a large book to someone they thought would be sympathetic, someone who respected the pope and was unafraid to write about sin.

"I still believe in the old faith," one of them said.

"The old faith? What faith?"

"I mean our faith before they started talking about love all the time. There was right and wrong and punishment. There was fear of God and the following of the law. Since Vatican II and the theology of love, everything has been watered down and made easy."

My heart went out to the men. But it was with sadness. "Well, when do you think the love stuff started? Don't you think Jesus talked about love?"

One of them said he knew there was a place for love, but in these days it had taken over everything and made a mess of the church. I felt depleted and tense after the meeting was over. It seemed that this good man had missed so much. Yet he was trying to reach for a truth that we all are somehow in touch with.

As for love, the Gospels and Epistles would fragment into a million pieces without it. Our saints would be incomprehensible, our heroes nonexistent. And Jesus would not be. "For God so loved the world that he sent . . ."

The following passage is from the First Letter of John, not the Second Vatican Council: "Love is of God. Everyone who loves is begotten of God and has knowledge of God. The person without love has known nothing of God, for God is love. Love, then, consists in this: not that we have loved God, but that he has loved us and has sent his Son as an offering for our sins." How could we imagine a Christianity before love became its center?

The love that this letter describes is not primarily our love of God, but God's love for us revealed in the offering of the Son for the forgiveness of our sins. It is the same love that Paul celebrates in the thirteenth chapter of Corinthians, the love from which, he writes in Romans, we can never be possibly separated.

Jesus, in the fourth Gospel, calls us to live in that love. How are we to do that? By keeping his commandments. Ah, finally the law, finally right and wrong. And what is his commandment? "Love one another as I have loved you." There is no escape. Our faith in Jesus is haunted by the mystery of love.

Perhaps this mystery itself is what causes us disquiet. Love, after all, is not easily won, rarely found, and never really earned. It also leads to improbable situations like that of the prodigal son and the lost sheep and to forgiveness for dreadful sinners.

This is, of course, not the narcissistic and self-indulgent state of mind that passes for "love" in contemporary life. Nor is it the great tidal wave of emotion associated with "falling in love." Rather it is, Paul reminds us, patience and kindness. It lets go of jealousy, conceit, and resentment. It delights in the truth. It trusts. It hopes. It endures. All of these qualities of love are attributes of God's love for us. What is more, love's greatest expression—to lay down one's life for one's friends—is what the Passion means.

None of this is new. And none of it is easy.

To have or not have rules can be easy. To keep or break commandments can be easy. We can set up our lives in such a manner that we allow no restraint or limit on our egos and desires. We can also legislate our lives so relentlessly that we delude ourselves into thinking that we have actually earned, produced, and now control the love that our scriptures speak of.

But the love revealed in Jesus, simple as it sounds, is terribly arduous. That is why the history of our faith so often reads like a history of our resistance to love.

Give us rules. Give us magic. Give us threats. Give us mighty victories in war or splendid successes in the marketplace to insure our worthiness. Give us Communion counts, converts, and the approval of the nations to guarantee our righteousness. But the mystery of love?

One of Dorothy Day's favorite passages from world literature occurs in Dostoevski's *The Brothers Karamazov,* where the old Father Zossima points out to Madame Hohlokov that her supposed crisis of faith is really a crisis of love: "For love in action is a harsh and dreadful thing compared with love in dreams. Love in dreams is greedy for immediate action, rapidly performed and in the sight of all. . . . But active love is labor and fortitude, and for some people too, perhaps a complete science."

No, love is not as easy as we may think. And its challenge to us is certainly nothing new.

29. The Contest of Faith

Acts 1:15–17, 20–26; 1 Jn. 4:11–16; Jn. 17:11–19

"The world has hated them for it."

Love is not easily given. Nor is it easily received. And yet the mystery of love is the heart of Christian faith. Its basis is, as the First Letter of John tells us, God's love for us.

This, for starters, is problematic. God's plan does not mesh with ours. Contrary to our hunch, our primary task is not to do good works but to believe in God's love for us revealed in Jesus Christ. Our faith in this love, the sixth chapter of John's Gospel tells us, is our fundamental work. When we work to believe in this gift, we accept our salvation. And once we accept it, we are empowered and sent to love others. The gist is this: "God loves you, Johnny, so be good," not: "Be good, Johnny, so God can love you."

Messages like this can irritate us, especially if we are self-made men and women. We prefer to earn our gifts and grace. Having achieved our salvation, we can then compare ourselves to others, those lesser people who do not make the grade, those publicans and prostitutes. We can also be jealous of those who seem to have gotten more than they deserve— laggards who came in at the eleventh hour.

An even more disturbing aspect of the gospel of love is that we are supposed to give it to other people. Freud, in *Civilization and Its Discontents,* called this notion singularly nonsensical. Even to love one's neighbor as oneself he deems absurd: "Anyone who follows such a precept in present-day civilization only puts himself at a disadvantage."

The harsh realities of life counsel us that if we love others, they will make a doormat out of us. In fact, the realist in us may suggest that Jesus himself was made a doormat. Had he used our methods, he would have grabbed the world by its neck. He would have mustered armies, enlisted geniuses, and aligned himself with bright strategists. He would have educated the elite and manicured the mighty. No such luck.

The reality principle of the world around us often has contempt for the mystery of love. Its scorn is revealed in those special insults: "You do-gooder," "you bleeding heart," "you good Samaritan," "you turn-the-other-cheek-er." The most telling ridicule the world heaps upon a believer appropriately slurs the gospel. Of course, "God so loved the world as to give God's only Son." But the world also rejects the Word made flesh—and his ilk.

Praying to the Father, Jesus says: "I gave them your word, and the world has hated them for it; they do not belong to the world, any more than I belong to the world."

As Christians, we are sent into the world as Christ was sent. We are an incarnate people. In terms of our civil societies, we are a people of inculturation. Our faith lives in and through the cultures we inhabit. Herein lies the splendid diversity of all the ways our faith is celebrated. The one mantle of baptism is arrayed resplendent in Leeds, Galway, Nairobi, Sante Fe, or Seoul.

But the Incarnation is also about realities beyond this world and its ways. It is a testimony to truths that extend further than the reach of the earth or any culture. This is why the world will hate the bearer of Christianity. Or at least it should.

Inculturation is not the same as "acculturation." To become acculturated is to capitulate to the wisdom, myths, and reality of a culture. It reduces the faith to a mere function of ethnicity or ideology, a mere handmaiden of revolution or capitalism. Faith must always resist acculturation, or it will have nothing to say to the world or to the culture. Acculturation tames faith; it makes it a lap dog for pop, rap, or politics.

Herein lies the conflict between faith and culture. Is our culture the last word on reality? Or is there some other truth, some other wisdom which defies our cultural wisdom and dogma? Many resist the possibility. "Face the real world, Father. Money talks. Power talks. If you can't accept the facts of life, you're not going to make it in this world." (Was Judas— the one who would be replaced by Matthias—just being a realist when he deserted the cause?)

Be realistic. "Everybody's getting a little on the side. Everyone has a price. You have to look out for number one." Such are the dogmas of cultural indoctrination. They intimidate believers into submission. Cultures that wield such clubs will spurn the gospel and its bearers.

So it happened in the Rome of the Caesars and the Florence of the Medicis. So it happened in Communist Russia and militarized El Salvador (what a strange combination of words). So it happens in capitalist America, where our young are taught that to follow the gospel is to be an unrealistic goof. The world which evangelizes hate will always hate the gospel of love.

Jesus knew this. He prayed for our strength and our protection: "Consecrate them by means of truth—your word is truth. As you have sent me into the world, so I have sent them into the world."

We would have settled for an easier job.

30. Solidarity and Courage

Acts 2:1–11; 1 Cor. 12:3–7, 12–13; Jn. 20:19–23

"Not a spirit of timidity."

If Pentecost was the start of the church, it was a birth out of frailty. The believers were huddled in fear behind closed doors. Yet Pentecost unleashed a courageous power. Driven by wind and fire, the followers of Jesus were set loose upon the world to make bold proclamation.

The Spirit brought unity, not only in a shared sense of poverty and smallness, but in the common experience of one God in Jesus, one faith, and one baptism. It was a faith that also put believers in touch with their deepest humanity. They would now speak a universal tongue, in a way which could touch the hearts of people from Africa, Asia, the Middle East, and Europe.

Universality of scope and unity of heart would be hallmarks of this church in its truest moments—not only in its sense of itself, but in its reach over the earth. "There are different gifts but the same Spirit; there are different ministries but the same Lord; there are different works but the same God who accomplishes all of them in every one."

It is precisely the strength of unity that allows the church to embrace diversity. Without union in faith, the diversity makes no sense, for there is no common reality over which pluralisms agree. But with the power of union, separateness is overcome, plurality celebrated.

"It was in one Spirit that all of us, whether Jew or Greek, slave or free, were baptized into one body. All of us have been given to drink of the one Spirit." Our deepest union relativizes all distinctions and eventually subverts them. No longer is being Jew or Greek the primary distinction of life. No longer is being slave or free the dominant criterion of worth. Being one in Christ is.

The unity of faith in Jesus is a subversive power that overturns any particularist claim to supremacy. Since Christ is our primary reality, his Spirit is a force that liberates us from any bondage other than our bond in faith. We are empowered by the Spirit to resist.

Thus, the second theme of Pentecost is courage. The earliest church was made bold in its proclamation of the truth. Believers' hearts filled with the good news of Christ, they were set on fire with love and zeal.

The fourth Gospel portrays Jesus as promising the advocate who would guide his apostles through their relationship to the world in matters of truth, right, and judgment. The Spirit of truth will give them courage. "In the world you will have trouble, but be brave: I have conquered the world" (Jn. 16:33). After Jesus invokes the Spirit advocate, he offers his great priestly prayer, bequeathing to his followers not only unity, but a fearless devotion to the truth.

The author of the Second Letter to Timothy takes up the refrain: "That is why I am reminding you now to fan into a flame the gift that God gave you when I laid my hands on you. God's gift was not a spirit of timidity, but the Spirit of power, and love and self-control" (1:6–8).

An intense sense of unity and an equally intense mission were not only the first fruits the early church received from the Spirit; they are also gifts we urgently need today.

It is no secret that division within Christianity is still a major scandal to the world. We may not be assaulted by religious military wars, but we still have our battles. One can find non-Christians remarking on the irony that Catholic priests have been perceived as leaving their parishes and people so that they might marry in another Christian church. And this irony is matched by other Christian clerics who are perceived as leaving their communities for Catholicism in hopes of avoiding women priests. Whether the perception be true or not, what a terrible indictment it would be if our relationship to God and church came down to married or women clergy.

If one left one's Christian community for reasons of faithfulness to the gospel, or to separate oneself from a people scandalous in its treatment of the poor, it might make some sense. But to reject either celibacy or women at the altar?

And this is only one of the issues that not only fragment us, but debilitate our mission. The more we ignore our one faith, Lord, and baptism, the less we feel capable to address our world, the less we have anything to say to the world, much less say it boldly.

If we are bereft of a strong sense of unity and purpose, with what do we confront a culture that has enthroned enlightened self-interest? With what do we challenge a world that has reduced men and women to pawns of ideology? With what arms of virtue and belief do we address the heartbreaking slaughter in Rwanda and pogroms conducted by Serbs or Croats?

In our own postmodern way, we are still the pre-Pentecost church, huddled in fear of each other as well as of the world at large. How true it is that we long once again for the "lover of the poor, the light of human hearts, the kind guide and giver of gifts, the gracious visitor who eases our toils, the consoler with cool grace and light in darkness, the warmer of our hearts and healer of our wounds, the gift of joy and absolver of sins."

Send forth yet again your Spirit upon us to renew the face of this troubled earth.

31. At the Bottom of Reality

Dt. 4:32–34, 39–40; Rom. 8:14–17; Mt. 28:16–20

"The voice of God speaking."

Walker Percy, in *Lost in the Cosmos,* mused ironically about the strange fate of postmoderns who spend millions trying to get chimps to talk and billions on space stations attentively listening for an extraterrestrial blip that might speak to us.

Meanwhile, we are sheepish about the possibilities of a personal God and positively skeptical about whether God has anything important to say to us. More strange still, humans wonder whether they have anything meaningful to say to each other. We, like God, seem impoverished in this age of personal deconstruction. Some high-priced academics even pontificate that there is no author, there is no text.

At stake are answers to questions about the universe. What is at the bottom of things? Is it the grind of impersonal machinery doomed to the laws of entropy? Is it the endless cycle of nature marked by convulsion, evolutionary chance, and final stasis?

The Moses of Deuteronomy answered thus: "Did anything so great ever happen before? Was it ever heard of? Did a people ever hear the voice of God speaking from the midst of fire, as you did, and live?" The absolute not only had a voice. It was father and mother to us, protector, nurturer, and guide. We were not the mere effluvia of silent aeons or an excrescence of the cosmos and its earth. We were God's children.

Paul wrote to the Romans that our response to the universe and its origin was not slavery or fear before the impersonal forces of matter and history, but an "Abba" to an adopting parent. We are full heirs to the God who need not have made us so, but freely chose to enter most intimately into our lives. Perhaps this is why adopting parents portray in a pre-eminent way the utter gratuity and generosity of a God whose life would be lavishly showered on us.

We Christians, with our Jewish and Islamic brothers and sisters, encounter a God who speaks. But what particularly marks our faith is the way our God speaks and what is spoken.

In Jesus, we worship a God whose word is expressed in human flesh. And what is revealed is this: our God is a relational being, a personal reality. In God there is a mutuality of knowing and loving, of being known and being loved. As persons, with our own insatiable desire for knowledge and love, we are adopted into this interpersonal reality of God and called to share it with others.

"Full authority has been given to me both in heaven and on earth. Go therefore, and make disciples of all nations. Baptize them in the name of the Father and of the Son and of the Holy Spirit. Teach them to carry out everything I have commanded you. And know that I am with you always, until the end of the world."

This commission to the apostles at the end of Matthew's Gospel, although probably a later addition to the earliest texts, is a trinitarian formula, much like the Pauline references to "Spirit, Lord and God" in both letters to the Corinthians. It is found in doxologies from Justin to Saint Basil and represented in prayers and artifacts from the second to the fourth century. It would not emerge as a full-blown "one God in three Persons" trinitarian doctrine until the end of the fourth century. Devotions and eucharistic feasts would emerge in France and Italy during the eighth and ninth centuries. And Thomas Aquinas, in the thirteenth, gave it an exquisite theoretical expression. This was all before Rome approved a feast of the Trinity in 1331.

Today, it marks our ancient baptismal formula as well as our eucharistic greeting: "May the grace of our Lord Jesus Christ, the love of God, and the fellowship of the Spirit be with you all" (2 Cor. 13:13).

The long, historical unfolding of our trinitarian faith is central to a dramatic struggle over human meaning and destiny. It is a strategic player in the grand competition for our minds' allegiance.

Are "itness," "thingness," matter, and force the ultimate categories of existence? Or is there something else? Someone else? Someones else? Is the cosmos mute? Or does it address us as the voice of God?

Percy ends his *Lost in the Cosmos* with a fantasy that spaceship Earth is indeed addressed by an extraterrestrial being. A persistent signal questions us:

> Repeat. Do you read? Do you read? Are you in trouble? How did you get in trouble? If you are in trouble, have you sought help? If you did, did help come? If it did, did you accept it? What is the character of your consciousness? Are you conscious? Do you have a self? Do you know who you are? Do you know what you are doing? Do you love? Do you know how to love? Are you loved? Do you hate? Do you read me? Come back. Repeat. Come back. Come back. Come back.

Our celebration of the Trinity is not only a credal affirmation that a community of persons is at the bottom of existence. It is also a remembrance of our source and goal: the personal God from whom we came, the God who calls us back home.

32. An Embodied God

Ex. 24:3–8; Heb. 9:11–15; Mk. 14:12–16, 22–26

"This is my body."

We believe in a God incarnate. The fact that the eternal Word was human flesh in Jesus of Nazareth centers our faith.

Hence Christians, and especially Roman Catholics, seem to celebrate the human body endlessly. We cherish sacraments that affirm God's presence in our births and dyings, our confession of sin, and marking of commitment. Our feast days are remembrances of deaths, births, and even conceptions.

Not only do we celebrate when Jesus was born; we commemorate those precise moments of space and time when he was conceived and circumcised. And after we honor the Holy Spirit and the Blessed Trinity at this time of the church year, our rituals turn to Christ's glorious flesh. We celebrate his heart as sacred, his blood as precious, and his body as transfigured.

Christians cannot be other than a people that honors the body. True, we are quite aware of its frailty and fate, but its ontological goodness remains an inescapable fact. Thomas Aquinas insisted that the body could never be the ultimate source or immediate cause of evil. Otherwise, how could the Incarnation have occurred? How could Christ have been a human body?

The feast of Corpus Christi—now called the Body and Blood of Christ—has had, over centuries, special associations. Its origins seem to be in the thirteenth century's cultic response to eucharistic controversies of the previous century. Until then, focus on the Eucharist centered on the sacrificial action of the sacrament rather than on the real presence apart from the Mass. As the reception of Communion became rarer among the body of believers, the impulse to adore from afar was intensified through devotion to the enthroned sacrament. The piety of holy men and women, including the likes of Aquinas, also called attention to the Blessed Sacrament until it became an official celebration of the church at the beginning of the fourteenth century.

Eucharistic processions were found as early as then. The great slow march of believers became a splendor of physicality, not only in solemn parade but also in a panoply of sensible delight: sound in song, color in vestment, fragrance of incense and flower.

Whatever its historical genesis and development, the feast of the Body and Blood of Christ has a thematic reach that touches the core meaning of our salvation and the furthest extent of our mission.

First, it is a celebration of Jesus Christ's body, a body like our own, genetically coded, conditioned by birth, developing through life, and undergoing the terrible relinquishment of death. It is a celebration of his body, moreover, which he identified with bread and wine in his Last Supper, given to us as the food of faith. We literally take into our own bodies the body of the Savior. This re-enacts the Incarnation: God once again takes human flesh. We are the indwelling.

Communion also re-enacts our redemption. Each time we celebrate this sacrament we embody the covenant of Christ, wherein God sees in us anew the flesh of Jesus. It was not by the "blood of goats and calves, but by his own blood" that our redemption was achieved and our consciences cleansed. Jesus Christ, "body, blood, soul, and divinity," becomes substantially one with our bodies as our very food and sustenance. Thus God beholds each of us and sees the beloved Son sent to save us.

But it is not only God's vision of us that is affected. Our own vision of ourselves and of each other is transformed. If we fully penetrate this mystery, we are empowered to see each other as God sees us: as the body and blood of Christ.

The consecration at the Eucharist is marked by the words, "This is my body. . . . This is my blood." Through our Communion, the words apply to each of us. Transubstantiation, then, applies not only to the appearances of bread and wine, it also applies to the appearances of human flesh.

Perhaps this is the eucharistic meaning of Jesus' parable of the last judgment in Matthew 25. When all the nations of the world are gathered together, the Son of Man utters those strange words: "Insofar as you did it to the least of these, you have done it to me." In the body of the prisoner or stranger, the hungry or the naked, the disconsolate or the sick, a second transubstantiation has taken place. Christ has said over the least of us: "This is my body."

In his sermon "The Weight of Glory," C. S. Lewis wrote: "Next to the Blessed Sacrament itself, your neighbor is the holiest object presented to your senses." Christ's body is as hidden in the least of us as it is under the appearances of bread and wine. Both require an uncommon and daring faith.

When we labor for human rights, when we shelter the poor, when we dismantle the bombs, when we protect the unborn, when we reach out to the criminal, we do these things not as political activists or social workers. We do them not as liberals or conservatives. We do them as people who worship the incarnate God.

The body and blood of Christ is not only our redemption. It is our task.

33. Imperceptible Life

Ez. 17:22–24; 2 Cor. 5:6–10; Mk. 4:26–34

"We walk by faith, not by sight."

A tiny sprig is planted. It becomes a mighty cedar to shade and shelter life.

We scatter seed on the ground. We sleep and rise day after day. Through it all, the seed sprouts and grows without our knowing how it happens. First the sprout, then the ear, then the ripe wheat.

A mustard seed, among the smallest of the earth, slowly rises and erupts. It unfolds to reign as the largest of shrubs, ample enough for birds to nest and hatch in.

The reign of God, this matter of faith, hope, and love, this kingdom for the ages, need not measure well in isolated moments. It is a living and growing thing.

So also our lives. Life is slow and subtle. Love takes time to show and grow. In life, little acts count. In fact, that is what a life is all about, a long parade of moments deceptively inconsequential.

Children grow before our eyes. But they age imperceptibly. We recognize growth only after it has happened. The full truth of the child is seen after the child is no more.

We ask ourselves: have we made progress? We are almost never aware of it. Only with effort and discipline do we become fully conscious. If we keep a journal, now and then we are startled when we peruse past entries. Worries, fears, preoccupations of the previous year seem to have evanesced. The greatest terrors and strongest urgencies of five years ago now surprise, embarrass, or encourage us. Was this me? Why was it that I could not gauge it as it was lived?

Life, like faith and love, resists most measurement. As it develops, it is rarely noticed. We seem not to do these things by sight. Our changings are unmarked as they happen.

This is why, perhaps, a daily examination of our awareness can be so life-enhancing. Examination applies the lens of believing to the blur of daily particularities. It is to notice in faith. It is to pay attention lovingly, gratefully.

Like sowers, we scatter our activities, our tiny acts of faith, flung out far and profligate, some taken by the wind, all landing somewhere. We sleep our nights and do our days, and the growth takes place. We may not even be conscious of the flowering.

Sometimes, by the grace of journey, whereby we depart and then return, we suddenly come to see the child now strong and true, the sapling broad and expansive.

But journey outward is not the only way to understand the present. In a journal, we move inward. We penetrate the present with conscious faith and love. We remember our destiny in Christ so that it might inform each present moment and quicken it with slumbering life. The import of life's every day, as St. Paul suggests, is revealed "at the tribunal of Christ."

"We continue to be confident. We know that while we dwell in the body we are away from the Lord. We walk by faith, not by sight."

34. Incomprehensible Death

Job 38:1, 8–11; 2 Cor. 5:14–17; Mk. 4:35–41

"Does it matter to you that we drown?"

A little over a year ago, Sister Ann Manganaro died. On Trinity Sunday I heard her last words: "God help me." And the swirling undertow pulled me down. Why death? Why any death? Especially the death of one who had loved so well and true.

She was a Sister of Loretto, a physician, a poet. Only in her mid-forties, cancer would sweep her away. Away from the people she served in Guarjila, El Salvador, away from her Catholic Worker friends and family in St. Louis, away from the people who needed her healing powers, away from the faces who looked to her grace.

Job, in the midst of the storm of life, called out for an answer to the chaos he felt. And God replied to Job: "Who shut within doors the sea and clothed the clouds as babies in blankets?" That's that. Who was Job to question the unnameable and most high? And what do all of our complaints about death amount to?

Strongly as his quarrel with God may still haunt our thoughts, we Christians have a fuller answer to our questions than Job did. We have Jesus, sleeping, yet with us at sea. He sleeps even though the turbulence is close to flooding us. Finally he speaks up, only to chide us—almost as heartlessly as God did Job: "Be still. . . . Why are you so terrified? Why are you lacking in faith?"

Our faith is not a guarantee that we will not go under. But it is a promise that, even if we nearly drown, Jesus will be with us. Not every storm of ours is miraculously silenced before his command, but all can be transformed by the abiding presence of love that disarms all fear.

This is not a mere human judgment, Paul warns us: "The love of Christ impels us. . . . He died for all so that those who live might live no longer for themselves, but for him who for their sakes died and was raised up."

The love of Christ is the object of our faith. It is not reducible to rational or utilitarian calculus. And yet it recasts the greatest absurdities that batter our minds.

As a neonatal intensive care physician, Sister Ann once took care of a five-inch premature baby named Tamika. The girl was left in the hospital, fated to die, unable to thrive, bereft of possibility. She smiled once, cupped in Ann's hands, after weeks of being held, caressed and gazed upon. Then she died.

After we two buried Tamika with the help of a generous funeral director, I protested to Ann that it all felt so meaningless and bleak. "What on earth did Tamika ever have?"

"Well," Ann said, "she had the power to evoke love from me."

And so it would be with Ann, just hours before she died, with all of her powers so diminished, her lively mind so quiet, her loving actions now gone. All that was left of Ann was what she shared with Tamika: the power to evoke our love. And God's.

"Anyone in Christ is a new creation. The old order has passed away; now all is new."

35. Prophetic Dying

Wis. 1:13–15, 2:23–24; 2 Cor. 8:7, 9, 13–15;
Mk. 5:21–43

"The favor shown you by Jesus Christ."

St. Paul's message of grace is about Mev Puleo. I first met her when she was a college student—vivacious, intelligent, and wonderfully on fire. There was a splendor to her joy. Energy sparked her writings, her talk, her photographic genius. Later, in the hope that others might see her work, I proposed a book called *Faces of Poverty, Faces of Christ*—my words, her pictures worth a thousand words.

This was only a small part of her labors. Mev was a theologian, like her husband, Mark Chmiel, at the Jesuit School of Theology in Berkeley, California, and her photography graced journals and newspapers. She attends to the poor, especially of Central and South America. She reveals their faces. She records their voices.

But now it is Mev who is poor. She who was rich, as St. Paul writes, "in every respect, in faith and discourse, in knowledge, in total concern," is powerless before the threat of death. Her brain hosts an incurable malignancy allowing only a 40 percent chance of living three short years. The poor now must speak for her.

The night before her surgery she was told that Gustavo Gutiérrez sent not only his prayers, but the prayers of all the poor. Thus we, too, are included, so poor before the mystery of life and death.

If God does not make death or rejoice in it, then why does God not cure her? The Book of Wisdom claims that God fashioned all things that they might have imperishable being. But we perish. All of us. And now Mev Puleo seems scheduled—far too soon. Justice may be undying and love may be eternal, but she faces death.

So pray I must. Our world, our church, our people, her friends need her too much. Jairus said to Jesus: "My little daughter is critically ill. Please come so that she may get well and live." Fate was reversed. Why will you not heal Mev? Is she not as worthy as Jairus's child?

And so I concocted a plea for a miracle. I summoned advocates, her favorite inspirations—Oscar Romero, Dorothy Day, and Sister Ann Manganaro. Her family would enlist medical means. All of us would besiege heaven.

When I read the prayer to her over long-distance lines, she requested one change—the addition, "if it is according to your will." And so it read:

"Good and gracious God of all the heavens and the earth. In Jesus Christ, our savior, our brother and your Son, you have revealed the healing power of your love and your will that death be overcome. We pray that, if it is according to your will, your glory shine forth in the miraculous healing of Mev Puleo's incurable brain malignancy. With the intercession and solidarity of your servants Dorothy Day, Archbishop Oscar Romero, and Dr. Ann Manganaro. We ask this through Jesus Christ our Lord. Amen."

Mev's additional words were her reminder to me that Jesus said: "Fear is useless, what is needed is trust." God wills that we not perish. In faith more supple than mine, she knows that even if we die to this world, we may trust God's will that we live eternally.

36. Prophetic Living

Ex. 2:2–5; 2 Cor. 12:7–10; Mk. 6:1–6

"My grace is enough for you."

Most of us know the old definition of an "expert": anyone who comes from more than fifty miles away. By now, the requirement must be five hundred miles. We seem to have a problem with closeness, with the ordinary, with the everyday.

Expertise is most respected when it comes from a distance. Prophetic gifts as well. Prophets are best when they are far away and long ago. Here and now is a different story. "Surely she cannot be a prophet. I went to school with her." "He cannot prophesy; I know his mother." "That guy cannot be a source of grace and joy to others; I've been with him in community for years. He tells terrible jokes and wears cufflinks." Is this why no one is a hero to one's own valet?

We reject not only the prophets around us. We reject the prophet within. This is the repression of the prophetic and heroic impulse of that person who is most ordinary and familiar to us: one's very self.

Since we are most often our own valets, most often familiar to ourselves, we are skeptical of the possibility that we ourselves could be prophetic or heroic. We leave little room for prophecy in the spaces closest and most intimate to us. Thus, there is little room for the miracles of faith. "No prophet is without honor except in that person's native land. Jesus could work no miracle there, apart from a few, so much did their lack of faith distress him."

In the tradition of so many other reluctant prophets, we use our proximity to ourselves as our excuse. "I am too young, too unprepared, too old, too weak and sinful, too busy and preoccupied, too homely, too nice. If only I could fly to a far-off place and some other time, in disguise, armed with stirring rhetoric and bright virtue. If only I could seize the pulpit or get the ear of the bishop, or be a holy subversive in the college of cardinals. Then, then I could prophesy."

But not here. Not now. Not me.

The reason we reject our own heroic and prophetic possibilities, if we are honest with ourselves, is that we know how weak and inadequate we are. Surely a hero cannot be lurking behind such common talent, such ordinary appearance. Surely a prophet's life is not marked by failures and frailties such as ours.

St. Paul, it seems, was also hounded by the thought of his inadequacy. He begged—three times—that God would remove the "thorn in his flesh." The prayer seems not to have been answered.

But if, like him, we learn to be "content with our weakness, for the sake of Christ," we may one day find ourselves unleashed, our hearts emboldened, our words firm and free.

"For when I am powerless, it is then that I am strong." If that is the case, all prophecy, like all politics, is local.

37. The Burden of Baggage

Am. 7:12–15; Eph. 1:3–14; Mk. 6:7–13

"Take nothing on the journey."

When I went to India several years ago, I lugged along a load of books that I wanted to read during the sojourn. It almost broke my back, hauling that stuff around. And yet, at least at first, how I treasured my books. I carefully underlined and highlighted the passages that would come in handy someday.

But the books weighed on me. Not only were they hard to carry, they were heavy on my time. When I heard of a Jesuit who had converted thousands of men and women, animists from Bihar, I started to give away my precious burdens. The wiry missionary, in response to the question of how he had touched so many people, simply said: "I travel light, so I have time. Any distance shorter than twenty miles, I walk, so I have time."

As my pack of wonderful books shrank, my back got better. And I had more time to live.

I must not have learned my lesson very well. I remember laughing at myself more recently, as I prepared to spend a year in Africa. My packing was meticulous: the right shoes, plenty of underwear, aspirin and antibiotics, a short-wave radio to get the BBC, more books (but fewer than I took to India), and a mosquito net.

Quite a different scenario from the one presented in Mark's Gospel. Jesus sent the disciples out, two by two, with nothing for the journey but a walking stick—no food, no traveling bag, not a coin in their purses. Sandals were proper, but no second tunic.

I realize, of course, that we are in a different time. And it is appropriate to take things on our journey to help us in our efforts of healing, blessing, anointing, and preaching. But it is an uneasy accommodation. More often than not, the excess baggage hinders rather than helps.

We Christians—bishops, priests, and people—in our manifold ways are all called to be disciples, often as healers and teachers, sometimes as reluctant prophets like Amos. But I wonder if we carry too much baggage.

It's not merely the things we stuff in our luggage or carry along with our entourage. It may be all the excess trappings of our power, privilege, and money. It may be crusty ideology and pet theories. As an old woman from North Saint Louis used to say: "I'd rather see a sermon lived than talked."

A Christian, whether pope or peasant, is most effective in discipleship when least ambivalent in motive. It is so easy to skim the benefits off the top. It is so tempting to serve the good news of our own egos and prominence, rather than yield to the harrowing truths we preach.

If we profess that "it is in Christ and through his blood that we have been redeemed and our sins forgiven," then perhaps our lives could be lived a little more simply, a little less ambiguously. It might be more evident to others and ourselves that it is indeed Christ we are made for, not the trappings we carry.

With too much baggage, it is our baggage we serve, our own nests we feather. Could this be why some of our apostolic efforts in the world today seem ineffective? Could it be that we are more skilled at collecting our benefits than shepherding the faith?

38. Jesus No Boy-O

Jer. 23:1–6; Eph. 2:13–18; Mk. 6:30–34

"You have driven them away."

Every once in a while, my uncle in Galway, Ireland, would refer to a particular type of priest as a "boy-o": "Yeah, he was a real boy-o." After many visits to his farm and endless badgering, my uncle finally told me what he meant, reluctant though he was to say anything disrespectful of "the priests."

A boy-o was the kind of priest who, if he saw that you had two fine geese, would say, "That's a fine goose you have there," and expect the other to be delivered to his door on the morrow. A boy-o always made you feel like an imposition, so burdensome were his tasks. A boy-o came to be served rather than to serve. A boy-o could cause people to fear and tremble in their pews, if they ever entertained an idea other than his own. A boy-o could divide a parish, humiliate a sinner, and even make you wonder about God.

My uncle was a truly gracious and uncomplaining gentleman, but a boy-o seemed to get under his skin. It was a good thing he did not have the temperament of Jeremiah. "Woe to the shepherds who mislead and scatter the flock. . . . You have driven them away." Jeremiah rebukes the shepherds who care more for themselves than their people. God will regather the flock and bring them back with new shepherds who will teach them not to fear and tremble.

Our own days have been marked by reports of shepherds who have abused our young. The headlines sadden and outrage. But lesser sins of the shepherds are known as well. Some Catholics have felt lost after leaving the confessionals of the past. Others have had their rosaries ridiculed, their piety chided, their childhood beliefs passed off as superstition. Mature and gifted laity have reported the strange experience of being treated like children or—in the case of women—like nonentities. Others have found their faith tried by perfunctory Eucharists, meandering homilies, and gripes about money.

Mere instances—not prevalent, I hope—but reminder enough that Jeremiah speaks to our day. Shepherding is a daunting and treacherous task, not only for church leaders, but for all parents and every giver of care.

Lest we get disheartened, the manner of Christ is instructive. He is gentle with his bunglers: "Come by yourselves to an out-of-the-way place and rest a little." And he is compassionate toward the people. "He pitied them, for they were like sheep without a shepherd; and he began to teach them at great length."

Let them never forget, those who are shepherds, what the teaching is all about, what the message means, what the church is for, what life amounts to: "It is he who is our peace, and who made us one by breaking down the barrier of hostility that kept us apart. In his own flesh he abolished the law with its commands and precepts, to create in himself one new man from us who had been two, and to make peace, reconciling both of us to God in one body through the cross which put enmity to death."

He was not a boy-o.

39. The Bread of Life

2 Kgs. 4:42–44; Eph. 4:1–6; Jn. 6:1–15

"What good is that for so many?"

This week's scripture begins a series of eucharistic controversies that will haunt the Gospels over the next four weeks. I wonder if it is a strategic gift of providence.

The *New York Times* has reported that almost two-thirds of American Catholics believe the consecrated bread and wine to be "symbolic reminders" rather than the body and blood of Christ. This seems a little startling, even if it was unclear what the respondents actually meant by "symbolic reminder" or "body and blood."

For some people, the word "symbol" can indicate the most sacred of realities. For others, "body and blood" has to mean actual physical properties. Even this year, for example, I encountered a young Catholic who thought the sacred host, if cut, should bleed.

Regardless of the exact interpretation of the questionnaire, I think the *Times*-CBS poll does reveal a challenge to contemporary faith.

There certainly seems to be a lack of reverence, now and then, for the reality taking place at the liturgy. A university student, intelligent and gifted in leadership, observes that he wished fellow students would give as much attention to their dress and appearance for Mass as they do for a date or job interview. An old priest, after a Mass in the infirmary, thanks me for genuflecting before the Eucharist. After a high school Eucharist, one of the theology teachers advises me to put consecrated hosts into a bin to be consecrated again the next time.

The problem of reverence, however, is nothing new. In the pre–Vatican II church, there were at least some priests who gave Communion as if it were a fast-food option. It is also not merely an American phenomenon. Perhaps the most unreverential distribution of the Eucharist I have been a part of was in Rome, where the hosts were delivered rapid-fire like quarters from a fist.

We naturalists and materialists are ill-fitted for miracles and transcendence. We seem unable to handle much more than appearances and style. Deeper realities are suspect. But if this is so, not only will real presence and transubstantiation seem improbable to us. Creation, redemption, resurrection, sin, and grace will seem so as well.

It is wonderful that our Eucharists have become more immediate, understandable, and participatory since Vatican II. But perhaps the cost of making it understandable has been the embarrassing realization that the Mass, if we actually believe what it proclaims, is uncomfortably miraculous.

If Christ really has given us the Eucharist, he is doing something far greater in our midst than Elisha's feeding of two hundred with twenty barley loaves or even Jesus' own stupendous feeding of five thousand. What we will find in the subsequent passages of John's Gospel is Christ's promise to become our very bread. In faith we hold that this promise is not some mere human symbolic projection. No, we are witnessing the holy of holies in our very midst.

Many may still be skeptical. For those who believe it, awe is only appropriate.

40. The Bread of Labor

Ex. 16:2–4, 12–15; Eph. 4:17, 20–24; Jn. 6:24–35

"Working for perishable food."

We work for food. We work hard. We get money for our work. And money? It has been known at times as "bread." In fact, an advertisement for the Missouri lottery consecrates the miracle of winning as "our daily bread."

We work for salvation, too. We produce, we practice virtue, we follow the rules, we do the required. Sometimes this allows us to think that we actually earn it all.

Still, we die. We perish. The things that sustain us perish with us. All of the earth goes back to the earth. All the physical bread, having once fed us, feeds the rest of the food chain. The old self, Paul reminds us, deteriorates through illusion and desire.

But Moses spoke of another bread. It would not fill the stomach like the diet of Egypt's fleshpots. It would be manna from heaven, God's promise, sheer gift, always there like snow on the ground.

Jesus in the fourth Gospel is portrayed as warning us not to work for perishable food. There is another kind of bread, the bread of our destiny, a "food that remains unto life eternal." The people asked Jesus to perform a sign that they might believe in him. The eternal bread would be his sign—the new manna, the new bountiful gift of God. Jesus himself is to be our sustenance, and that is the work of God. "I am the bread of life. No one who comes to me shall ever be hungry; no one who believes in me shall thirst again."

This is not easy to believe, to say the least. It demands a great effort for us to let go of the illusion that we can ultimately feed or save ourselves. But this faith is precisely what Christ requires of us.

When the crowd asks Jesus what they must do to perform the works of God, he makes it very clear: "This is the work of God: have faith in the one God has sent." Our vital labor as Christians is nothing other than our working to believe that Christ is indeed our bread of life, our sustenance.

If there is any pre-eminent task for us as we celebrate the Eucharist, then, it is not that we execute it well or work out our different roles, helpful as these things may be. Our task is to believe that our God, in Jesus, is our very food and drink.

The liturgy is not just a meal we have made, not just fellowship, not something we have artistically dreamed up. Its reality does not depend upon our ingenuity or virtue, our expertise in preaching or singing. It is fundamentally an act and gift of God.

Our act and gift in return is to receive it, to be nourished by it, to believe it.

This is not an easy task, our faith. And our generation is not the first to balk at Christ's promise to be our real food. "How can he give us his flesh to eat?" This was the response that many made to him.

We too, in our own days of discipleship, when it is difficult to believe so lavish a miracle, are invited to offer a response.

Such is our work at hand.

41. Sustained

1 Kgs. 19:4–8; Eph. 4:30–5:2; Jn. 6:41–51

"I myself am the living bread."

Strengthened by God's sustenance, Elijah, even though he felt like dying, walked forty days and nights to the mountain of the Lord. Such is the bounty of God.

We too are beneficiaries of God's miraculous nourishment. It is the eucharistic sign of Jesus. "This is the bread that comes down from heaven, for you to eat and never die. I myself am the living bread. . . . If you eat this bread, you shall live forever; the bread I will give is my flesh for the life of the world."

A mighty claim. God would be our food, our ultimate provision. God actually wants to inhabit our flesh, make us tabernacles. And think what a powerful profession of faith it is to believe this. Our "Amen" is a radical assertion of dependence and desire. "You are our food and drink. You are our sustenance. You are what nourishes us."

The people around Jesus knew just how radical the matter was: "Do we not know his father and mother?" "Is this not Jesus, the son of Joseph?" "How can he claim to have come down from heaven?" The appearances confound them. How can it be? He is familiar. How is it possible? He is commonplace. How can he be from heaven? He is flesh and blood like us.

The Eucharist, like the Incarnation, is a scandal to empirical observation and technical reason. If that is our bottom line, we may as well forget all matters of faith. Forget the matters of hope and love as well. Even the exhortation of Paul—that we be forgiving, compassionate, and imitators of God in our love—is sheer mindlessness if only seeing is believing.

Our contemporary struggle with belief in the real presence of Jesus in the Eucharist is a quarrel over transcendence. Only the here is real. Only the now is actual. Only the observable is knowable. Only perishables can sustain us. The immediate feeling. The experience at hand. The pain pressing. The pleasure welcome. Our problem is not just believing that God could inhabit bread. It is believing that God could inhabit us.

We have trouble believing anything transcendent about ourselves. "Can anyone ever say 'forever,' anyway? Is there anything possible left of us after our body decays? Is there anything more to us than satisfactions of power and money?"

It may be arduous for modern minds to believe the proposition that God could be our food and drink. It is just as difficult to believe anything wonderful about ourselves, to hope that there is anything more to sustain us than matter chewed, drunk, and digested.

And yet our faith is just that—faith. Faith that there is more than surface and superficiality. Faith that the transcendent takes flesh. If somehow we have become locked in a state of mind in which the "real presence" is impossible to accept as a gift of God, nothing wondrous will be possible for us. There is no point to the journey, no answer to the quest of our minds, no final satisfaction for the hunger of our hearts.

Twentieth Sunday in Ordinary Time

42. Nurtured

Prov. 9:1–6; Eph. 5:15–20; Jn. 6:51–58

"Taste and see the goodness of the Lord."

Wisdom offers herself as our food and drink, a table spread for us, a banquet: "Come, eat of my food, and drink the wine I have mixed." True wisdom nourishes the whole person. It empowers us to leave foolishness and deception behind.

Ephesians portrays the Spirit as the real answer to our thirst. Quenched, we no longer "act like fools and wallow in ignorance." The Spirit inebriates; it does not debauch. It unlocks the voice in grateful song: "Give thanks to God the Father always and for everything in the name of our Lord Jesus Christ."

But what is true wisdom? What is real fulfillment? More basically, what is real? These questions are the hidden agenda in Jesus' encounter with the crowds in the fourth Gospel. His claim is this: "My flesh is real food and my blood real drink."

And real food and drink are what "real presence" and "transubstantiation" are all about in our sacrament of the Eucharist. What is at stake is what we believe to be most real in our lives. What is true nourishment? And what words best designate the real and true?

It so happens that in our own history, influenced by Greek categories and various refinements of medieval philosophers like Aquinas, the word "substance" has been linked with reality. "Substance" indicated the deepest reality that abides through all flux of external appearance or change. To say that the Eucharist involved "transubstantiation" was to say that the reality of the consecrated bread and wine, despite appearances of color and material composition, was the "body, blood, soul, and divinity" of Jesus. The "real presence" of Communion was Jesus Christ in his full mystery. He is the sustenance of our lives, the nourishment of our faith. He is our truest food and drink. "I myself am the living bread come down from heaven. Anyone who eats this bread shall live forever; the bread I will give is my flesh, for the life of the world."

Those who heard him speak these words objected to them: "How can he give us his flesh to eat?" And the objections still go on, even as we trudge our way into the twenty-first century.

Although the category of "substance" may not be the issue, real food is. What, indeed, is our real bread and drink—in the most profound sense of the word "real"?

We find in the Gospel for next week that, after Jesus spoke of these things, many of his followers rejected his teaching. "This is intolerable language. How could anyone accept it?"

When some of his disciples abandoned him, he asked the Twelve: "What about you, do you want to go away too?" And Peter said: "Lord, to whom shall we go? You have the words of eternal life."

The question abides. What about us? Do we too want to go away? Are the words too hard for us? Or might we be inspired by the great song of long ago: "O food of wayfarers, O bread of Angels, O manna of heaven-dwellers. Feed those who are hungry. Do not deprive of sweetness the hearts of those who seek you."

43. Difficult Passages

Josh. 24:1–2, 15–18; Eph. 5:21–32; Jn. 6:60–69

"This sort of talk is hard to endure."

"How can you take these words seriously?" This question in the Gospel is actually a complaint about Jesus' claim that he is food and drink, but it serves as a wry comment on the passage from Ephesians heard before the Gospel. Talk about words hard to endure!

"Defer to one another out of reverence for Christ. Wives should be submissive to their husbands as if to the Lord because the husband is head of his wife just as Christ is head of his body, the church, as well as its savior. As the church submits to Christ, so wives should submit to their husbands in everything. Husbands, love your wives, as Christ loved the church. He gave himself up for her. . . . Husbands should love their wives as they do their own bodies. He who loves his wife loves himself."

"Does it shake your faith?" It probably shakes many of us. Deference and reverence, first of all, are not prominent nouns in our contemporary lexicon of privileged words.

More troublesome yet, "wives should be submissive to their husbands." This sounds like fingernails on a blackboard. Feels like sandpaper on wounds. Tastes like abuse. Smells like patriarchy. Submission has been the problem. Why pose it as a solution?

Clearly there is a hierarchical context for Paul's words to the Ephesians. Christ is compared to the husband, the church to the wife. The man is the head; the woman the body. This analogy has been acclaimed by some, who want to legitimate the privileged imaging of the male for Christ. But it has been roundly condemned by others, who see it as a devaluation of women. Both positions are worth examining, but what is the real theme of the Ephesians text? "Deference" and "reverence" are its context. All the rest is application. We must all defer to and revere one another. Then Paul provides applications that may or may not be historically bound.

But it is deference we have trouble with, "submission." It sticks in the craw. Why should any of us have to submit to another or put someone else first? What is worse, Paul seems to commend obedience only to the woman. He tells the wives to be submissive. What about the men?

Well, what about them? This is what Paul says: Give yourself up for her. Love your spouse as your own body, your very self. If husbands were to hold such an attitude, it would subvert all dominance and hierarchy. Paul's is a radical statement of equality, albeit in his own contemporary context. It is self-destroying to abuse, hurt, degrade the spouse.

The point is this: there may be suggestions of male dominance in our second reading today, but this conclusion collapses from internal contradiction. Both husband and wife are to put the other first.

What if this rankles us the most? The very idea that we must give ourselves to another, defer to another! If we love each other as we propose, we assuredly must die to ourselves. The first casualty of real commitment is the imperial ego we are so reluctant to tame.

"Decide today whom you will serve." In marriage, as in life, we serve not only each other, but our very God, who wants of us not slavery, but the free gift of our love.

44. Disturbing Words

Dt. 4:1–2, 6–8; Jas. 1:17–18, 21–22, 27;
Mk. 7:1–8, 14–15, 21–23

"This people pays me lip-service."

The fornicators among us are surely going to be disturbed by Jesus' words. So also the greedy-guts. The same might be said for liars, adulterers, thieves, killers, sensualists, the envious, the arrogant, and the obtuse.

Perhaps the best tack is to scrap the whole Gospel and talk about love or expansion funds. It is not uncommon, after all, for us to expunge those parts of the Gospel that offend us. But usually we have to listen to the stuff and squirm.

It is a funny thing to sit in the pew on Sundays when a whole list of sins and sinners is enumerated from the Gospels or the various Epistles. Our shoulders shrink a bit in hope that we are not mentioned, or at least that the blows fall not too hard. Possibly we feel relieved that smoking and drinking are not mentioned. Some of us may sigh. It is those "others" that Jesus is talking about.

Or maybe we dwell—savoring it—on those "others." That guy who has loads of money. I hope he heard the word "greed." Or the woman who has seen three marriages. She'd better be listening. Or those fakes who think they are so good; they'll get their fill of this Gospel. And I hope those people who eat and drink too much know what the word "sensuality" means. They could learn a thing or two if they would just open up their ears. As for those who envy my own virtue and success, thank God they are condemned as well.

The old Pharisees were experts in the law. Matters of right and wrong. Weighty concerns of judgment. They knew where people stood. But Jesus seemed to have more difficulty with the Pharisees than with any other group. They did not mind hearing about sin, as long as it didn't apply to them. They were righteous, but self-righteously so. They honored their self-images and projections, their own traditions. Jesus quoted Isaiah to penetrate their defenses: "You teach as dogmas mere human precepts."

For myself, this stings a bit. I cherish what has been handed down as tried and true. But if I cherish tradition, must I not be vigilant that my heart is in the right place? Does Christ speak to me when he says: "You disregard God's commandment and cling to what is human tradition"? Does he address his church? Its scribes? Its leaders? "This people pays me lip-service but their heart is far from me. Empty is the reverence they give me because they teach as dogmas mere human precepts."

A secret consolation is this: if our hearts are stung by Jesus' challenge to the Pharisees, our hearts are almost healed.

A gifted and forceful woman once told me of a horrifying revelation. She realized at prayer that she was the Pharisee, she who judged others, she who did not trust God.

What a lovely moment. If you think you are a Pharisee, you most surely are not. If you think you are not, watch out.

45. "Faith, Yes, But . . ."

Is. 35:4–7; Jas. 2:1–5; Mk. 7:31–37

"Did not God choose the poor?"

It is Christ who saves us, yes, not our works. And it is by faith in him that we accept salvation. But this does not mean that all our other actions count for nothing. The authenticity of our faith is tested out by the fruit it bears, particularly in our relations to each other—more particularly still, in our relationship to the poor. The Letter of James is not unique in stressing action. Most of the words attributed to Jesus do the same.

Concern for the poor and marginal is not a pet theory fabricated by liberation theologians or some left-wing ideology. It is as old as Isaiah: "Say to those whose hearts are frightened, be strong, fear not. . . . The eyes of the blind will be opened . . . the ears of the deaf be cleared." Our God is concerned with the fate of those visibly wounded and at the margins of life.

The Letter of James makes it even more clear. It speaks of our ritual assemblies. How do we relate to the members of our congregation? Let us imagine an immaculately dressed man in designer clothes, or a gilded superstar with gold on neck and fingers. Then we see a bag lady, a little confused, in shabby clothes, maybe murmuring to herself. To whom do we attend? Whom do we wish to win over? Whom do we avoid?

"Suppose further you were to take notice of the well-dressed man and say, 'Sit right here, please,' whereas you were to say to the poor person, 'You can stand.' Is this not a corrupt decision?"

Ouch! The writer then reminds us that God chose the poor in the eyes of the world to be rich in faith and heirs of the kingdom. Unfortunately, we often choose only the rich to make them a little poorer for the sake of the building program.

As for Jesus in the Gospels, there is no doubt he accepted and loved rich and healthy people, especially those who knew their own wounds and poverty. But he always had time for the marginal and the dispossessed, the maimed and the broken. If we were to measure the amount of space in the Gospels devoted to the hurt or poor and compare it to any other pet issue we cherish as the "litmus test" of our faith, there is little doubt that the sick and needy are more important than any other reality.

Witness Jesus in the Gospel of Mark. He attends to the deaf man, a passive mumbler. He draws close. He touches him and prays. And his power shines forth. If we say that we are disciples of Jesus, if we hold that he is not only our savior but our way as well, then his manner of concern must in some way be our own.

Our attentiveness and care for each other and especially for the poor is not a tactic to win us paradise. It is rather our grateful response to God's promised love for us in our own poverty and disability.

Perhaps this is why it may well be the old bag lady in the back, so marginal to the world, or the quiet penitent near the door, reluctant to approach the altar, who brings a greater gift of prayer than any of us laden with talent or largess.

Twenty-fourth Sunday in Ordinary Time

46. Faith Doing Justice

Is. 50:4–9; Jas. 2:14–18; Mk. 8:27–35

"Faith that does nothing in practice."

What good is it to profess faith without practicing it? Such faith has "no power to save." The writer of the Epistle is very clear. Faith may be the central response in our relationship to

God; but faith, like love, must find expression in our actions if it is to be real.

If I see someone starving and, making a quick getaway, bless that person with "Good-bye and good luck," I have a faith problem. To say, "I hope you keep warm and well fed," but to do nothing to help others in their bodily needs, is to have a thoroughly lifeless faith.

There are parts of scripture I may want to reject. "You cannot mean this. You will never demand this." Yet faith does have its demands. It makes claims on us. Its implications are daunting.

The challenge faith puts to us in relating to the poor is no more scary than its challenge to the ways we relate to God. There is a pain in the heart of Christian faith itself, since its object is the mystery of God's love revealed in Jesus' death.

When the journey of faith seems too arduous, when we have "compassion fatigue" before the sea of human suffering, when it seems we are not even up to believing in Christ anyway, it is good for us to remember the struggle of poor old Peter.

Jesus, recall, asked his disciples, "Who do you say that I am?" Peter then makes his great act of faith in Jesus as the Messiah. But immediately after Jesus says that he will suffer and be put to death, Peter resists the implication of his profession of faith. "You can't be asking us to accept the cross." Jesus rebukes Peter. "Get behind me, Satan. You are judging not by God's standards, but human ones."

Now that would be enough to stop me in my tracks. Not only is Christ asking the impossible, but when I simply bring up the problem, he rebukes me and calls me a "satan."

But Peter simply "gets behind" Jesus and keeps following, no matter how confused he may feel or how impossible the task may seem. He still follows—in his inadequacy, in his failure, with all the limitations of his merely "human" way of thinking.

The poor will always be with us. So also will the physical and moral evils that make them so. Our efforts are dwarfed before their immensity.

Our faith as well far outdistances our capacity. It asks, in effect, that we somehow give up our very lives, embrace the cross that Christ himself bore, and follow him.

In the end, it is not our task to end the sin and suffering of the world or to stop the mindless march of violence. It is, rather, to follow a different way: to take opportunities, small as they may be, to reduce hatred and carnage, to let go fears, and to entrust even our poor inadequacy to the hands of God. This is the taking up of our daily cross.

TWENTY-FIFTH SUNDAY IN ORDINARY TIME

47. Perils of Power

Wis. 2:12, 17–20; Jas. 3:16–4:3; Mk. 9:30–37

"Inner cravings make war."

Why murder? The question has haunted me these months. It is difficult enough to face the deaths wrought by impersonal forces of nature, the wear of time, or the frailty of bodies. But murder. The will to kill. The choice to exterminate a human being—this roils the mind.

1994 is a murderous year. Perhaps they all are. But the killing fields of Bosnia, irrigated by ethnic cleansing, were more than matched by the slaughterhouse of Rwanda. All the labors of the years—the schoolchildren, nurses, nuns, priests; the buildings built and people trained; the families started and commitments made; the neighbors welcomed and babies nourished—all obliterated in this Christian, predominantly Catholic, country.

An estimated half million persons were killed in little over a week's time. These men, women, and children were murdered, not by bombs or antipersonnel weapons but by hand-held clubs and knives. It is incomprehensible that such brutal devastation could be brought by ordinary people upon their friends and fellow believers.

But as further reports mounted, the logic of murder was presented with greater clarity. I had to face the question myself: what would I do if the price of staying alive, of protecting my home and family, was the hacking to death of the family next door?

"We were forced to move with the killers in order not to be killed," a teacher was quoted in the *New York Times*. "It was just a way of protecting myself. We risked being killed." Another account presented the fatal choice: "A drunken vicious gang confronts me and says that if I do not hack to death the family next door, my family will be executed. In the end, my loved ones, my autonomy, my land are at stake." And so the "patho-logic" mounted. Is this the logic of all murder?

As Christians, whether we live in Rwanda or Philadelphia, we employ a different logic, a different wisdom. The Letter of James says it is a wisdom "innocent, peaceable, lenient, docile, rich in sympathy and kindness." It yields a harvest of justice, sown in peace. Conflict, however, arises from the logic of inner craving that yields a war within us and around others: "What you desire you do not obtain, and so you resort to murder."

The problem is we desire to live, to be free, and to make a family and home in peace. What if these are threatened by a monstrous world? What if, to be alive and loving and free, we must take the life and love and freedom of the neighbor in the next yard or the neighboring country?

Anyone whose faith is radically Christian is at a terrible disadvantage. Everything, even our deepest attachments, is put at risk—especially when we confront a monstrous threat. "With revilement and torture let us put him to the test that we may have proof of his gentleness and try his patience. Let us condemn him to a shameful death; for according to his own words, God will take care of him." So the wicked plot, Wisdom reminds us.

And so it would be with Jesus, who was "delivered into the hands of men to put him to death." Ultimately Christ refused the logic of power and self-preservation. He entrusted his entire being into the hands of the One who sent him. And three days after his death, he rose.

Are we to follow him in entrusting our lives and loved ones to God even if it means sure death? Are we to believe that there is more to our existence than our deepest human need for survival?

Perhaps the depth of our Christian faith makes too terrible a demand upon us. Perhaps it did for the Christians of Rwanda. A Lutheran minister admitted that to prove one was not on the side of the victims, "you had to walk around with a club. Being a pastor was not an excuse. They said you can have religion afterwards." The aftermath brought a horrible realization to this man of God: "I haven't found the answers. There are times when you lose faith. Sometimes we think God has abandoned Rwanda and allowed the devil to enter the souls of our people."

Underneath the logic of murder, however, is not only the gaping abyss of God's absence. There is also a void of faith, hope, and love—even for ourselves. An infinite hole yawns at the bottom of our humanity, when we admit that in our hearts is a desire that can lead us, yes, even to slaughter the innocent in defending our own. Commentators have not been far off in opining that the carnage of Rwanda somehow represents a total loss, not only of religion, but of any moral, social, or humane order.

To be sure, there were heroes. We have already heard the stories of men and women who resisted even to the extent of being killed rather than killing, of neighbors who harbored and hid their friends at great peril, of families who departed a monstrous world rather than take part in it.

Yet a troubling conundrum haunts me: would I have done the same?

48. Perils of Wealth

Num. 11:25–29; Jas. 5:1–6; Mk. 9:38–48

"Come now, you rich."

Prophets announce future promise. They also unmask idols of the present. This is why they are resented, those "prophets of doom," "disgruntled grouchers spouting jeremiads." They sign up travelers for endless guilt trips. They rant uninvited and out of turn.

And so Joshua asked Moses to stop two upstarts from prophesying in the camp. These prophets had not been legitimized or approved. But Moses said: "Would that all the people of the Lord were prophets! Would that the Lord might bestow his spirit on them all."

We usually like prophets when they say what we want to hear. They are especially welcome if they heap indictments on our enemies. When they get close to home, it is a different matter.

A case in point: today's reading from the Letter of James. Has a wealthy parish ever heard the likes of it? Has a bishop ever dared to utter it without fear of being run out of town? "You rich, weep and wail over your impending miseries. Your wealth has rotted, your fine wardrobe has grown moth-eaten, your gold and silver have corroded, and their corrosion shall be a testimony against you. . . . You live in wanton luxury on the earth; you fattened yourselves for the day of slaughter."

Most priests and bishops know better than to try to get away with such stuff. If words like these are ever spoken, they are heard in the assemblies of the oppressed and poor—tirades against the privileged which the privileged, unless they read liberation theology, rarely encounter.

The problem of riches is one of the great secrets in capitalist Christianity. The truth would be too hard to bear. Popes and bishops might be padded in comfort, surrounded by silver and gold. And we ourselves are probably members of the wealthiest church in the most dazzling culture of the world.

Our television evangelizers are so intent on our money, they dare not condemn it. In fact, if you spend a month of Sundays listening to the preachers, it would seem as if Jesus never said a mumblin' word about money. Proclaimers of the gospel are easily trapped. As one very wealthy man once said to me: "You better not love the poor too much. If you do, who's going to give you the money to keep going?"

Money may be our biggest difficulty. Marx called it our "jealous god," who can tolerate no other deity. "Only in money will my soul be at rest, in cash is my hope and salvation. It alone is my rock of safety, my stronghold, my glory."

Money has immense power. It is almost sacramental. It gets us acceptance into the real world. It seems to clean the most vile acts. The very possession of it sanitizes us. The most loathsome behaviors are rendered "cool," if not splendid. Whether we are murderers, usurers, abusers of women and children, dope pushers, money can still get us limousines and drivers. No matter what we have done, hangers-on will mouth their "yes" to us, hoping for a tip, a nod of beneficence. It provides entry into the most select of clubs. It buys life and death, bodies and body parts. It purchases persons.

I complained once, while teaching at a university in New York, about *Indecent Proposal* (a movie wherein Robert Redford buys from a husband a night of sex with his wife for a million dollars). A savvy student tried to calm me down. "Relax. A million dollars? Most people would have sex with anyone for that, much less with Robert Redford in a snazzy Las Vegas hotel."

Maybe we should know better than to challenge the god-awful glory of the dollar. Maybe we should quietly ignore the seduction of riches. It is all too close and painful to us. It may even cause us shame. It is less troubling to join, surreptitiously, the conspiracy of silence.

And yet, what if our capitulation to the ultimate reality of money ties a millstone around our necks? What if our unwillingness to challenge its power dashes the deepest hopes of our young and "leads them astray"?

Jesus said some terrible words: "If your hand is your difficulty, cut it off." Well, what is our difficulty? What might be that thing we cling to more steadfastly even than our faith? Some of us might, indeed, be willing to cut off our hands for something we utterly believe in. But would it be for the sake of the kingdom that Jesus spoke of? Or only a million dollars?

Would that all Christ's followers were prophets, I faintly hope, in the words of Moses. Perhaps the moral bankruptcy of a capitalism which allows no moral or spiritual conviction to veto it would finally be unmasked for the pseudogospel it is.

If we contemplate such prophecy, let us prepare for resistance and, quite possibly, our own embarrassment. By all accounts we will be known as troublemakers and malcontents. Maybe so. But our young might imagine another world than the one where only "money talks."

They might imagine hope.

Twenty-seventh Sunday in Ordinary Time

49. The Two Shall Become as One

Gen. 2:18–24; Heb. 2:9–11; Mk. 10:2–16

"Let no human separate what God has joined."

I attended a wedding this summer. It seemed a special privilege, since I did not have to preside, or "do" the ceremony. The bride was a former student of mine, one of those young people you hold always as a luminous presence in your life.

It was beautiful in every sense: in its simplicity, in the strong words of the celebrant-homilist, in the splendor of bride and groom, in the families all gathered and garnered.

I thought of that wedding as I read this Sunday's scriptures. "It is not good for the man to be alone." Intimacy, relationship—the bottom of our being. "God took out one of Adam's ribs." Adam spoke, "This one, at last, is bone of my bones, and flesh of my flesh." The two of them became one body.

A psalm sings: "Your spouse shall be like a fruitful vine in the recesses of your home; your children shall be like olive plants about your table. Behold thus is a human blessed. May you see your children's children."

What act of great moment is remembered here? I thought of the young bride and groom. What was it that they wanted to say to each other and the world? They wanted to say "forever."

There is something that reaches the godly in such holy desire. When we abide in love, our hearts arch to the infinite. Rilke said, "Lovers, you touch pure permanence underneath."

Yet marriages fail. You'd think that fact alone might tame our dreams of forever. Yet I have never met an engaged couple who wanted to give their futures to each other "till it doesn't work out, till you get sick, till you go broke, till you break down."

What is it about us that wants to say "forever"? To say "eternally"? To say "till the end of time"?

Jesus was given a test by the Pharisees. It was a conundrum about eternal love and life. He asks them in return, somehow aware of their stubbornness, about the judgment of Moses, who permitted divorce. But Jesus digs down to the well of our hearts' desires. "They are no longer two but one flesh. Therefore let no man separate what God has joined." "Whoever divorces a wife and marries another commits adultery; and the woman who divorces her husband and marries another commits adultery."

It seems so clear and fast and abrupt. It seems even cruel to some who hear it. And surely painful. But isn't this always true with matters of love? Would any of us, bent on a life of covenant, settle for less?

Which brings us to the lapse of our loves, of our marriages. Some endings we call annulments (a term that others might deride; they say, why not call it a divorce—what it is—instead of pretending it is something else?). Others think that annulments are a farce, easily purchased, easily forgotten.

Well, they are not purchased, not a farce, and not easy. Just ask someone who has gone through one. An annulment is our own churchly attempt to deal with our own law, our own promises, and our desire to honor and obey Jesus as well as Genesis. It is not so much a judgment about our relationship to God (there are some divorced and remarried people, without benefit of annulment, who are, no doubt, far closer to God than the likes of myself, having never been married) as it is a statement about our relationship to each other and to our own intentions. We want to honor and respect our own words.

So an annulment process is an attempt to determine whether two people were, as a matter of fact, free and able to choose irrevocably in God to become "one flesh."

A divorce may mean many other things: that two who actually made an eternal covenant slowly grew apart, that they had irreconcilable differences, that one person could no longer abide another, or that they somehow never adequately and wholly chose to become irrevocably one. An annulment says only the last.

We Catholics have our liturgies, our communions, our Eucharists. Some of us attending are divorced and remarried and place it all before God, not knowing really whether we have put asunder what God had once joined in us. Some have annulments, a human judgment offered only after long analysis and painful remembrance. Some of us weep in the back, not approaching the altar of union. Some trust God and abstain. Some trust God and partake.

Few, thank God, judge. For no matter what our rightful relationship to our church, its laws and traditions, we all pray in an assembly of believers who are sinners; and, most assuredly, we all stand before our good and great God as children.

And Jesus spoke to the child in each of us. "Let the little children come to me and do not hinder them. It is to just such as these that the Kingdom of God belongs. I assure you that whoever does not accept the Kingdom of God like a little child shall not enter it."

"Then he embraced them and blessed them, placing his hands on them."

50. The Sadness of Many Securities

Wis. 7:7–11; Heb. 4:12–13; Mk. 10:17–30

"There is one more thing you must do."

What do we want more than anything else? What is behind the drama of our desire? What will make us happy?

These, of course, are the questions of philosophers and mystics. In quiet moments, after sudden joy or loss, they stalk our inner stillness. In creative moments, they launch imagination into soaring poetry and myth or the higher reaches of science and technique.

The courtly enlightenment in the Book of Wisdom echoes many of the answers that have cast their spell on human consciousness. Power and authority present themselves as escape from our dire contingency. Abundance of gold beckoned emperors and conquistadors. Health has monuments built to its promise: "If you have health, you have everything." Beauty has its troubadours and marketeers. Even the splendor of intellect impressed the Stoic as a way out of pain and insufficiency.

Yet there is a higher wisdom. "I preferred her to scepter and throne. And deemed riches nothing in comparison with her. . . . Because all gold, in view of her, is a little sand. . . . Beyond health and comeliness I loved her. And I chose to have her rather than the light, because the splendor of her never yields to sleep."

Abundance of riches, whether of mind, heart, or property, never seems to ease the hunger. We live in fear of losing our power, be it physical or mental. Money does not buy joy. Beauty, so skin-deep, lasts half as long. There are disenchanted intellectuals. There are "pictures of health" burdened with miserable lives.

Even success. Even if we somehow mount the pedestal of "self-made men and women," we invariably harden. We become consumed with our judgments about others who have not done as well with their endowments, we think. Amazed by our strength and success, we nevertheless are often puzzled why it is so difficult to encounter God, the plaything of our egos.

The higher wisdom is a deeper wisdom. Like God's very word, it "is living and effective, sharper than any two-edged sword. It penetrates and divides soul and spirit, joints and marrow; it judges the reflections and thoughts of the heart. Nothing is concealed from him; all lies bare and exposed to the eyes of him to whom we must render an account." Wisdom's word digs to the bottom of our existence. It spreads beyond the heights of our desire.

"What must I do for eternal life?" Our achievements are not enough. Our virtues are not sufficient. Even our keeping of the commandments seems not to still the question. We have kept all these things.

"Jesus looked at him with love." So he looks upon the longing of us all. He speaks: "There is one thing you lack. Go and sell what you have and give to the poor; you will then have treasure in heaven. After that come and follow me." At these words the man's face fell. He went away sad, for he had many possessions.

Somehow, the very things we keep, the gifts we cannot bear releasing, hold us in a grip of sadness.

There is a double melancholy here. We are sad at not being able to let go of all the assets we once thought protected us and ensured our safety; for we now know that what we imagined was security is somehow bondage. Our locks and guards have fastened us in.

Sadder still, we know we can never become safe enough, anyway. Try as we may to channel our infinite desires into retirement plans, we are haunted by our fragile bones and blood. There is no insurance policy strong enough to prevent death. No Rock of Gibraltar to secure us. No provident company that can prevent the pain of our humanity.

This is why it is so difficult for a rich person, a person with many securities, to enter the condition of blessedness. We must somehow become small, rather than big, to pass through the "needle's eye."

Whatever that phrase of Jesus means, it suggests an unnavigable journey, an impossible task. So who can be saved?

No one. Not by one's own providence and power. The only way to heaven is to let go of earth. The only way to life is to let go of the womb. When we are born, we fall into an even greater dependency. Life is harrowing and precarious, compared to the comfort of the womb. So it is that to be born into eternal life we must loosen our tight clutch on all the securities and gifts we hold so dear.

It is almost impossible for a man or woman secure in rich endowments to understand such mysteries. What need, after all, is there to call upon the God who made us, the God for whom all things are possible?

For the poor, whether in things or spirit, it makes lovely sense.

51. Lording It over the Rest

Is. 53:10–11; Heb. 4:14–16; Mk. 10:35–45

"It cannot be like that with you."

Most of us have heard of the contrast between "Christology from below" and "Christology from above." This opposition sneaks into most theological discussions, whether they are about dogma, scripture, morality, mission, or salvation.

Most of us are not theologians, but we can still sense what it is all about. The "above" emphasizes the divinity of Christ, the transcendent; the "below" emphasizes the full humanity of the Jesus of history.

Christology from above is the "old" way of thinking. It presumes that God, from above, enters history in Jesus, the eternal Word made flesh. Its strongest insights support our intuitive recognition of human inadequacy. It demands an admission that we are not enough. It calls for intervention and assistance from a reality beyond our own.

In its deficits, Christology from above so fixes on the divinity of Jesus that he looks like some kind of organic automaton, manipulated by a divine nature that knows everything in advance and feels nothing in actuality. All is fixed, tidy, and predicted. All is planned, neat, and efficient. Jesus is so utterly different from us, so remote and unapproachable, that we imagine him moved to compassion only by the pleading of his mother.

An equally oversimplified version of Christology from below stresses his humanity so much that you start wondering about that divinity stuff—whether Jesus pre-existed as the Word, whether he did miracles, whether he was raised from the dead, among other things.

It is easy for us to foul it all up, especially since we have big problems with notions of "from above" and "from below." Those who are above are the top dogs. They call the shots. They lord it over the rest of us. They pull the strings. When we feel below, we tend to resent those above. Or wish we could get to their status. Then we could dominate. Then we could control things.

Most of our notions of authority are rooted in this supposition. Those who have it, lord it. They take the first place. They put us in our place. Those who do not have authority easily resent it or hunger for it. (If only we could call the shots.)

There seems to be a strong tendency, consequently, to resist the authoritative aura of Jesus—although almost everyone who encountered him acknowledged his authority in word and deed. If we have nagging suspicions about "aboveness," we may insist on a Jesus from below. Little that we are, it is not pleasant to imagine anything greater than us. We love the below—as long as it can aspire to greatness and power. Even Jesus could make it as a self-made man.

Paradoxically, Jesus was very unlike us—both in his aboveness and his identity with our lowliness. Not only is he unlike us in being God, he is unlike us in being human. After all, we tend not to be very good at being humans, much less gods.

We construe our humanity in terms of mighty aspirations. But the human Jesus aspired to smallness. Oddly, even his divinity sought to be emptied out.

The Letter to the Hebrews reaches for this paradox. We have a "great" "high" priest. But he was strangely compassionate, fragile, and subject to the very trials we abhor. Isaiah warned of the fact. This savior would be afflicted, would suffer, and would even bear guilt. We want no afflictions, no suffering, and will admit no culpability. "For we do not have a high priest who is unable to sympathize with our weaknesses, but one who was tempted in every way that we are, yet never sinned."

This is a strange fix. Like Zebedee's sons, we aspire to sit at his right and left, but we do not know what we are asking for.

It is a cup of pain and suffering. It is an emptying-out. It is a descending.

The great joke on us is that the mighty God above goes down below, even below us, proud of ourselves for not needing anything other than ourselves.

What would it be like if we exercised our aboveness, our authority, in the manner of the God we profess to believe in? "You know how among the Gentiles those who exercise authority lord over it them: their great ones make their importance felt. It cannot be like that with you. Anyone among you who aspires to greatness must serve the rest; whoever wants to rank first among you must serve the needs of all. The Son of Man has not come to be served but to serve—to give his life as a ransom for many."

People in authority—even the churchly kind—may love exercising it. But they mistake the authority, the aboveness of God. If we feel excluded from authority, we may crave it. But we misunderstand the authority of Jesus.

Those who are above should go below. So it was and is with our God. Those who are below need not hunger for the heights. We need only enter more deeply into what we are, our humanness, to receive from the One above the message that even in our smallness the grandeur of love is revealed.

THIRTIETH SUNDAY IN ORDINARY TIME

52. The Terror of Love

Jer. 31:7–9; Heb. 5:1–6; Mk. 10:46–52

"Nothing whatever to fear from him."

I was once invited to give a series of meditations to a group of sisters who were new novices in a rather strict—some would call it conservative—community.

I made an early mistake. One of the first things I proposed to the young gathering was my conviction that fear was not the best way to approach God, especially if we are followers of Christ. In fact, I said, it seems that fear has very little place in our relationship to God.

As we see in the prophecy of Jeremiah, God wants us to shout for joy. We are delivered, gently gathered from the ends of the earth, with all the others of our motley kind, neither seeing straight nor walking tall. We may have had our tears, but our God wants to console and guide us, to lead us to refreshing waters. God is a parent to us. What use is there to fear a parent unless that parent is not very good? And surely God is good. We are like God's "firstborn." Why would we live in fear of God?

Even our great high priest is portrayed in the Letter to the Hebrews as someone who disarms our fears. He is not some unapproachably bombastic Wizard of Oz, before whom we cringe and crawl. No, "He is able to deal patiently with erring sinners, for he himself is beset by weakness."

One of the novices who was subjected to my ruminations had many reservations about my criticism of fear. "We should work out our salvation in fear and trembling," I was told, with a quotation from St. Paul. "Fear of the Lord is one of the great gifts of faith," another said.

I unfortunately took the challenge. "Well," I said, "let's take the week to look through the Gospels and the Epistles and find out how much fear is recommended to us and how much it is not."

I thought I would surely come up with twenty passages advising love and trust for every one promoting fear. And right I was. "Fear not" is a constant refrain, from the moment of the angel's visit to Mary all the way to the risen Lord's visit to the timid Apostles. In fact, I made a strong case that even the passage in the Letter to the Philippians about "fear and trembling" made little sense without the redeeming death of Jesus that St. Paul commemorates in the immediately preceding lines of chapter two.

Things did not go well. Somehow, it caused a storm. It seems there were long discussions over the intervening week about this problem of fear. I had pressed my point too strongly. And the novice director did not like my minimizing the virtue of "fear of the Lord." I was not invited back.

Perhaps it was for the best. For, although I feel quite confident at times about my experience of Jesus and the foolishness of fear, often I just seem to grope in the dark.

But even in these times, the story of Bartimaeus (does that really mean "son of fear"?) comes to my rescue. He was a blind groper, sitting by the side of the road. And all he could say was, "Jesus, Son of David, have pity on me." It is a prayer of last resort, the kind that supplies my words when there is nothing left to groan or claim.

Bartimaeus summoned a courage that many of us lack. To make matters worse, the people around him scolded him. They tried to shut him up. But he yelled out all the more, "Son of David, have pity on me!"

This persistent, bold trust must have stopped Jesus, who ordered his people to call the blind man over. Then the crowd changed its tone: "You have nothing whatever to fear from him. Get up. He is calling you."

The best instincts of history's Christian crowd echo the refrain. There is nothing to fear from him. And yet we halt. We had better wait. What will he ask of us? How might we be properly prepared to enter his presence? How can we be worthy to approach him?

The great, sweet punchline of this story is given to Jesus. He does not ask for fear or virtue. He does not demand righteousness or rectitude. He simply asks, "What do you want me to do for you?"

Now, what do you make of this God-man we worship, the savior we drink and nourish ourselves by? He loves our faith— he cherishes our trust—more than all our quivering fear.

I do not know whether the novices I encountered had

found a greater wisdom than I proposed. After all, one cannot presume to constrain the great and good God.

But my hope remains. In every blindness I may have, may I, begging for pity, bring it to the One before whom I have "nothing to fear." May I have nothing other to offer than my faith. May my hope surmount my fear. And may he say to me, thank God, "What do you want me to do for you?"

53. Wholeheartedness of the Saints

Dt. 6:2–6; Heb. 7:23–28; Mk. 12:28–34
Rev. 7:2–4, 9–14; 1 Jn. 3:1–3; Mt. 5:1–12

"First of all the commandments."

October is a great month for saints. It begins with the commemoration of St. Thérèse of Lisieux and ends with All Hallows Eve, the night of spirits who do not so much haunt streets as inspire hearts.

October is a month of giants: Francis of Assisi, who rebuilt the church and inspired centuries of holy souls; Teresa of Avila, mighty doctor of the church and reformer of the Carmelites; Anthony Claret, missionary, founder, archbishop of Cuba, and chaplain to the Queen of Spain; Simon, Jude, and Luke, apostles and evangelist; Ignatius of Antioch, one of our earliest bishops, a martyr in Rome; Margaret Mary Alacoque, Visitation contemplative, who with her Jesuit friend Claude La Colombière bequeathed the Sacred Heart devotion to the church.

Talk about diversity.

Yet they all had in common the kind of wholeheartedness that the Book of Deuteronomy and the Gospel of Mark require: to love the Lord our God with all one's heart, soul, mind, and strength.

At first hearing, the "Great Commandment" might suggest to us, as it did to a young woman at the turn of our own century, a range of high and mighty acts:

> all the deeds I long to accomplish for you. I would be a martyr, a doctor of the church. I should like to accomplish the most heroic deeds—the spirit of the crusader burns in me. I long to die on the battlefield in defense of the holy church. I would be a missionary. I would choose to be flayed like St. Bartholomew, plunged into boiling oil like St. John, or like St. Ignatius of Antioch I would be ground by the teeth of wild beasts into bread worthy of God. With St. Agnes and St. Cecilia I would offer my neck to the sword of the executioner, and like St. Joan of Arc, I would murmur the name of Jesus at the stake.

And yet Thérèse Martin, psychologically and physically frail, hidden and protected from the onslaughts of the world, soon realized that her gift was not that of the noble warrior or the martyr of faith, nor that of an apostle, missionary, or preacher. Her grace was to love with whatever heart and mind were given her.

The wisdom shared by all the saints, after all, was not about the particular talents or deficits one brought to the world. It was about the wholeheartedness of love, a willingness to give it all away. They also seemed to know that wholeheartedness was not a matter of "once and for all," or something that would happen overnight. It was, rather, a matter of opening up their entire lives to the transforming grace of God.

The little Thérèse would learn to love despite countless slights imagined or real, suffocating caregivers, and the frailty of her body and psyche. The great Teresa would face victories and terrible defeats, rewards and rejections—but with a permeating faith, even through disillusionment over projects and performance. Francis of Assisi suffered nerve-wracking discouragement and disappointments with himself and his communities. The wonder of their lives was that even in their defeats they abandoned everything into the care of God.

We imagine that wholeheartedness is some achievement or jewel of ours that we bestow upon the grateful Almighty. Or we fear that if we offer our all, something cherished will be snatched away from us. Too much might be asked. Something terrible demanded.

We miss the point. Wholeheartedness means that we present everything of ourselves before our God, even our dust and dross. The gift is not taken away, it is transformed. We are not robbed, we are revitalized.

Rabindranath Tagore, the great Bengali poet, in his *Gitanjali* tells the story of a beggar going from door to door asking for alms. He suddenly sees his celestial king approaching in a chariot and dreams of bountiful gifts and lavish endowments showered upon him by his liege. But to his surprise, the king asks him what he has to give. He stares, confused and undecided. But finally he peers into his sack of meager possessions, takes out a tiny grain of corn and gives it to the king.

"But how great my surprise when at the day's end I emptied my bag on the floor to find a least little grain of gold among the poor heap! I bitterly wept and wished that I had the heart to give thee my all."

All the saints, whether celebrated or unknown, would not cry bitter tears but weep for joy. Placing every grain of hope in God, they became likened to God. And in poverty or mourning, in gentleness or hunger, in the mercy they gave and the peace they brought, even in the terrible losses they endured, they found the happiness we all long for.

Saints have entered into the mystery of Christ, described by Karl Rahner as "the unique case of the perfect fulfillment of human reality (a nature which, by giving itself fully to the mystery of fullness, so empties itself that it becomes God) which means that humans only are when they give themselves away."

54. When There Seems Nothing Left

1 Kgs. 17:10–16; Heb. 9:24–28; Mk. 12:38–44

"All she had to live on."

I met John in 1975. We arrived the same day at the L'Arche community in Bangalore, India. It was a group home for handicapped people, founded in the spirit of Jean Vanier, the inspiration of many thousands around the world.

John was handicapped. I, so I thought, was not. John was a rarity, a forty-year-old man with Down's syndrome. He was frightened and withdrawn. It was the first time he had been away from his home and his mother, who had taken care of him over the many years. Now, since his mother was about to be hospitalized for a long time, John needed help and L'Arche was there.

As for myself, I was a little depressed, although it probably did not show. My own disability was covert—a lingering ache of disappointment. I had traveled to India, made a thirty-day retreat, and discovered that I was not changed at all. Still insecure, despite the degrees; still dissatisfied, despite the hoops maneuvered; still timid, despite big dreams. No Francis Xavier here.

Although not relating much to anyone for the first few weeks, John gave himself a job. He would sprawl on the floors, put his cheek against the concrete, and start blowing with all his might in wide arches. He was cleaning the dust from the hallways. He seemed pleased and proud of his contribution.

I contributed by cooking once in a while and presiding at the Eucharist, feeling quite valuable. But at night I would lie stiff and sleepless on my cot, hearing strange sounds on the other side of my unlockable door: a troubled teenager who would growl, sniff, and murmur as he peeked in; a gentle old man, talking and humming to himself after a day of simple chores; an urgent voice down the hall.

Neither of us Johns, I suppose, was doing very well, although the staff—"assistants"—worried more about him since he was less adept at covering up his affliction.

After weeks, a breakthrough occurred. John did it. Had he read my anxiety and protective distance? Had he sensed my wish that staying there would come to an end? Did he know I needed help?

One morning, as I made my way across a large room, stepping around obstacles, my leg was grabbed. John was on the floor "sweeping," face to the ground, yet pulling my ankle.

When I looked down, stopped and startled, I saw his released hand now motioning in the air as if he were shaking hands with a ghost. I was the ghost—but no longer, after I took his hand to shake it and saw his upturned face smile.

Why do I always think of John when I hear of the widow's mite? "She contributed more than all the rest. . . . They gave from their surplus. She gave from her need, all she had to live on."

I guess it was the power of his gift to me. His reaching out, even though by all accounts he had far less reason to do so than I. He had lost home and mother, familiarity and comfort. And somehow he still gave a gift to me.

I started feeling in happier spirits after that day. John did too, perhaps from sensing his own power to help another person.

Elijah met a poor widow of his own. He just wanted some water. The widow, gathering sticks, went to fetch it for him. Then he just wanted some bread. But there was nothing. She was gathering the sticks to make a fire. Left only with a handful of flour and a few drops of oil, she prepared a final meal to eat with her son before dying. "Do not fear," the prophet said. "Do as you were planning, but give me some as well. You will not run out." The three of them were able to eat for a year: the prophet, the woman, the child. The flour did not vanish. The oil did not go dry.

There are times when we are down, and we think we have nothing left to give. Little remains in the barrel of our lives. Then, for some reason, we still manage to give more out of the nothing we have left. And grace is born again.

How often the mere pennies of others replenish us. It happens in those moments when someone seems to have nothing much to give us: no education, no program, no sermon, no sound advice, no solution to our problems. If they do not give up on us, but give us something else, if they give not from their surplus, but all they have to live on, we find that they have offered their very being. Their presence. Their hearts. What they bestow on us, finally, is no merely human asset, but the life of God flourishing in our faith, hope, and love.

I heard about John for at least another five years. Once I even saw his smiling face in a little publication of the L'Arche community. I was told he was a joy of the community.

He helps me see why Christ was so touched by a widow one day, near the temple treasury.

55. The End Times

Dan. 12:1–3; Heb. 10:11–14, 18; Mk. 13:24–32

"You do not know the hour or the day."

As the church year was coming to its end, so was the life of Father Vince O'Flaherty. A Jesuit priest in his seventies, he started his last morning by offering the Eucharist at Regis High School in Denver and preaching on the "rich young man." As so often before, he would soar and inspire, speaking in a rough voice that, unexpectedly, was able to communicate a gentle vulnerability before the world and God.

Regis was his assigned community of Jesuit brothers; but in many ways his heart was with the community of his dreams, where he spent two or three nights a week—a little cluster of Regis University students living in the Denver barrio at a house called Romero. Spun out of the hopes of Father O'Flaherty and two younger Jesuits, Father Kevin Burke and the novice Mike McManus, Romero House brought together a handful of men and women in their early twenties who would not only study, but pray, live simply, and labor for justice together.

It was in that house that he died—after a day, no doubt, of visiting and being visited by friends, of talk small and profound with his little community, of faithful and warm counsel, of fond laughter and remembrance. He died of a heart attack in his sleep. No one, not even he, had anticipated the hour or the day.

Father O'Flaherty loved music, and the passion never left him. Even in recent years he would gravitate to a piano, pulled by the least request, and say, "Well, I'll sing only four show tunes."

He had been a soldier in the Second Great War and he regularly reknit the fabric of warm friendship by visits to old buddies and their wives.

As a Jesuit, he had been a novice and tertian director, a superior of communities, a spiritual guide, and steadfast companion to hundreds. Through all the years, he seemed to relish each day, whether it brought anguish that would wake him at night during his middle years, or turbulent questions in the 1960s and 1970s, or imaginings of a "great American novel" when he faced an older age, or earth-shaking changes for church and the Society of Jesus, or toasts to triumph and jubilee.

So what does this have to do with the word of God on the second last Sunday of the year, the week before we celebrate Christ the King?

Well, Vince O'Flaherty's life was an interpretation of the text.

Our summer over, the harvest upon us, God is near now, at the door. We envisage Mark's portrayal of the end times to be about the end of the world, the trials, the omens, the shaking of the heavens, the Son of Man coming in clouds with power and glory upon the winds.

And yet, if we take it all so literally, the text has lost its meaning. Jesus said, "I assure you, this generation will not pass away until all these things take place." How many generations have now passed?

The trick is not reducing the word to a historical period. We must let it speak to every historical generation, including our own. After all, the end times happen to us all, not only to each of us in facing our own sundering death, but to all of us together as a generation that will pass into the mist of disappearing ages.

Conceivably, the text is not so much a warning about the end of the world as it is a commentary on living in it. This day, this moment, this life, is the time to bear the fruit. Another year hurtles by. Seize the day.

As our projects and pretenses mount, as our labors and tasks surround us, as our entertainment and doodling while away